BEST *of the* BEST
from
Calling All Cooks
COOKBOOK

The Most Popular Recipes
from the Four Classic
Calling All Cooks Cookbooks

BEST *of the* BEST
from
Calling All Cooks
COOKBOOK

The Most Popular Recipes
from the Four Classic
Calling All Cooks Cookbooks

COMPILED BY
AT&T TelecomPioneers of Alabama

PUBLISHED BY
QUAIL RIDGE PRESS
Preserving America's Food Heritage

Library of Congress Cataloging-in-Publication Data

Best of the best from calling all cooks cookbook: the most popular recipes from the four classic calling all cooks cookbooks / compiled by AT&T TelecomPioneers of Alabama. — 1st ed.
   p. cm. – (Best of the best cookbooks series and calling all cooks cookbook series)
   Includes index.
   ISBN-13: 978-1-934193-21-1
   ISBN-10: 1-934193-21-6
   1. Cookery, American. I. AT & T TelecomPioneers of Alabama.
   TX715.B4856134 2008
   641.5973–dc22   2008027372

ISBN-13: 978-1-934193-21-1 • ISBN-10: 1-934193-21-6

First printing, September 2008 • Second, March 2009 • Third, October 2011
Fourth, March 2012
Printed by Tara TPS in South Korea

Design by Cyndi Clark.
Cover photo by Greg Campbell.
On the cover: Southern Iced Tea (page 14), Okra Cornbread (page 30), Cornbread Salad (page 77), Squash and Pepper Sauté (page 90), Glazed Sweet Potatoes (page 104), Best-Ever Pot Roast (page 137), Butter Pecan Bundt Cake (page 184), Orange Slice Cookies (page 224).

QUAIL RIDGE PRESS
P. O. Box 123 • Brandon, MS 39043 • 1-800-343-1583
email: info@quailridge.com • www.quailridge.com

Contents

Our Mission

To provide rewarding community service experiences and fellowship opportunities for all of our employees, retirees, and their families.

To provide value to sponsoring companies by generating brand visibility, building teamwork, developing leadership skills of employees, and demonstrating the corporate social commitment.

To enable our Life Members to maintain strong ties to our sponsoring companies.

To be well-known as volunteers meeting a variety of community needs, with special emphasis on education.

AT&T TelecomPioneers

Preface

The *Calling All Cooks* cookbooks have been the most profitable venue for the Alabama Pioneers since the first edition was published in 1982. While the original *Calling All Cooks* continues to be the most popular, the other books have also found their way into many households.

Customers have praised the recipes found in all four *Calling All Cooks* cookbooks. In fact, people have enjoyed the meals prepared using these four cookbooks so much that the requests for a book that combines the "Best of the Best" recipes has been a constant refrain from many of these cooks. Thus, this book is the result of those requests.

Pioneers across the state submitted their selections of time-tested and proven recipes from all four books. These selections were compiled, sorted, and edited, and now grace the pages of this cookbook as a collection of the best recipes of the CALLING ALL COOKS COOKBOOK SERIES.

This compilation is possible due to the countless hours of work by many active and retired Pioneers over the past 26 years. We would like to thank every one of them for their dedication and tireless efforts. Numerous projects that benefit education and community organizations have been funded by the proceeds of these books.

An immeasurable debt of gratitude is owed a very special volunteer who has been at the heart of our organization for a very long time. Many projects, including the publishing of this book have largely depended on her dedication to the success of the Alabama Pioneers. She has made a difference in the lives of many people and continues to be a driving force in all of our endeavors. Pioneer Betty Willingham has given so much to so many. It is only fitting that we dedicate this book to her, as a small token of our appreciation.

It has been a joy working on this project with the "Best of the Best" Alabama Pioneers and the staff at Quail Ridge Press. We expect this book to be the next essential cookbook for every household.

Carolyn Cauthen, Chapter President 2008
Archie L. Blackmon, Chapter President 2009

Note from the Publisher

Quail Ridge Press was honored to be able to participate in the development and publication of the *Best of the Best from Calling All Cooks Cookbook.* We have long been familiar with the CALLING ALL COOKS COOKBOOK SERIES, as each has contributed a wonderful sampling of their recipes to the Alabama edition of our BEST OF THE BEST STATE COOKBOOK SERIES.

The down-home, family-favorites in the CALLING ALL COOKS COOKBOOK SERIES are exactly the kind of recipes we seek to preserve in our BEST OF THE BEST STATE COOKBOOK SERIES—recipes that have been developed and perfected over generations; recipes that are legendary within a family and are now being shared with other families.

Each cookbook in the CALLING ALL COOKS COOKBOOK SERIES has been reprinted many times. The total sales of all four titles exceed well over 700,000 copies. The cookbooks continue to be popular with young cooks as well as longtime cooks.

The AT&T TelecomPioneers of Alabama, the organization of employees, retirees, and families of the telecommunications industry in Alabama, are the force that have made the *Calling All Cooks* cookbooks the success they are. The Pioneers are all volunteers who have given their time and energy to a variety of projects and activities that enrich our community.

I speak for all of us at Quail Ridge Press in saying that we are proud to be a part of this new cookbook that offers the finest recipes from the CALLING ALL COOKS COOKBOOK SERIES. This new cookbook will continue to provide the Pioneers with the revenue that finances their worthy projects and will enable Quail Ridge Press to continue our goal of Preserving America's Food Heritage.

Gwen McKee, President
Quail Ridge Press
Brandon, Mississippi

Contributing Cookbooks

Calling All Cooks

Published in 1982, this 738-page book contains recipes that have been handed down from generation to generation. One of the most popular of the CALLING ALL COOKS COOKBOOK SERIES, this cookbook makes cooking fun. Makes a great wedding gift or nice gift to give someone heading out on their own. There is a saying here, ". . . your kitchen is just not complete without a Yellow cookbook." Now in its 19th printing, *Calling All Cooks* has generated more than 2.5 million in profits.

Calling All Cooks Two

The first edition of *Calling All Cooks* proved to be a huge success and prompted us to collect recipes for *Calling All Cooks Two*. Published in 1988, this 709-page book contains many new recipes. Now in its 6th printing, *Calling All Cooks Two* has generated more than $850,000 in profits.

Contributing Cookbooks

Calling All Cooks Three

Published in 1994, this 646-page book contains nutritional information for each recipe to help make better food choices when trying to monitor caloric/carb/fat intake. This cookbook contains an excellent variety of salads, desserts and main entrées. Now in its third printing, *Calling All Cooks Three* has generated more than $375,000 in profits.

Calling All Cooks Four

Published in 2000, this 575-page edition was created in appreciation of 75 years of Pioneering in Alabama. Containing all new recipes, this cookbook is quickly becoming one of our most popular books.

*B*everages and *A*ppetizers

1876
Bell's Centennial Model

"My word! It talks!" exclaimed Emperor Dom Pedro of Brazil when this early phone was demonstrated by Alexander Graham Bell at the Centennial Exposition in Philadelphia on June 25, 1876. One of the judges called the invention "the most wonderful thing in America." Bell's success with the telephone came as a direct result of his attempts to improve the telegraph.

Just three months prior, while working with fellow inventor Thomas Watson, Bell shouted, "Mr. Watson, come here. I want you!" after spilling battery acid on a transmitter. Watson, working in the next room, heard Bell's voice through the wire. Watson had received the first telephone call, and quickly went to answer it.

Yellow Fruit Punch

1 (48-ounce) can pineapple
juice
3 (6-ounce) cans frozen orange
juice (add water as directed
on can)
2 quarts water

½ cup frozen lemon juice, or
½ dozen lemons, juiced
1 (6-ounce) package dry
lemonade mix
2½ cups sugar
1 quart ginger ale

Mix well all ingredients except ginger ale; freeze. Remove from freezer; let thaw at least 3 hours. Before serving, add ginger ale. Makes 1½ gallons. Serves 50 people.

Hazel Campbell, Birmingham South Council (Book 1)

Hot Spiced Percolator Punch

10-CUP VERSION:
3 cups pineapple juice
3 cups cranberry juice
1½ cups water
⅓ cup brown sugar

⅛ teaspoon salt
1½ teaspoons whole cloves
1 stick cinnamon

30-CUP VERSION:
9 cups pineapple juice
9 cups cranberry juice
4¼ cups water
1 cup brown sugar

¼ teaspoon salt
4½ teaspoons whole cloves
4 sticks cinnamon

Combine juices, water, sugar, and salt in coffee pot large enough for number of cups making. Place spices in coffee pot basket; perk and serve hot.

Dot Beadlescomb, Birmingham Central Council (Book 1)

Spiced Tea Mix

2 cups sweetened orange drink
  mix
1 cup instant tea granules
1 large package lemonade mix

1¼ cups sugar
1 teaspoon cinnamon
½ teaspoon ground cloves
½ teaspoon ground allspice

Combine orange drink mix, instant tea granules, lemonade mix, sugar, cinnamon, cloves, and allspice in a bowl; mix well. Store in airtight container. Combine 1–3 teaspoons of mix with 1 cup boiling water for each serving. You may substitute sugar substitute for some of the sugar, if desired.

Betty Foshee, Decatur Council (Book 4)

Russian Tea

1 (9-ounce) jar powdered
  orange Tang
1½ cups Lipton Instant Tea
  with sugar and lemon
¾ cup sugar

1 teaspoon cinnamon
¾ teaspoon ground ginger
1 teaspoon ground cloves
¼ teaspoon nutmeg

Mix all ingredients and store in covered jar or container until ready to use. For 1 serving, place 1 or 2 teaspoons of mix in cup. Add boiling water and mix well.

Jewel Edney, Pat Goodwin, Riverchase Council (Book 2)

Sparkling Summer Tea

2 family-size tea bags
4 cups boiling water
1 (12-ounce) can frozen
   lemonade concentrate,
   thawed

½ cup sugar
4 cups cold water
1 (1-liter) bottle ginger ale
Lemon slices

Steep tea bags in boiling water in a pitcher 15 minutes. Squeeze tea bags and discard. Add lemonade concentrate, sugar, and cold water. Stir and chill in refrigerator. Add ginger ale and mix gently. Serve immediately over crushed ice. Garnish with lemon slices. Yields 14 servings.

Jo Ann Thomas, Selma Life Club (Book 4)

Southern Iced Tea

2 quarts boiling water
6 tablespoons loose tea
4 sprigs fresh mint

1 quart cool water
2½ cups sugar
6 tablespoons lemon juice

Pour boiling water over tea and mint in large container. Let steep, covered, 10 minutes. Stir in cool water; strain. Add sugar and lemon juice; mix well. Pour over ice cubes in glasses. Yields 15 servings.

Ray Foreman, Birmingham South Council (Book 3)

Very Bloody Mary

7½ cups tomato juice
¾ cup beef consommé
½ teaspoon Tabasco
½ teaspoon lemon juice
2½ teaspoons Worcestershire

1 teaspoon celery salt
1 teaspoon salt
½ teaspoon pepper
Vodka

Combine all ingredients except vodka; mix well. Fill each glass with ice and pour in 1 or more ounces vodka. Add mix and stir slightly. Garnish with a wedge of lime and/or celery stick. Makes 1½ quarts mix.

Larry York, Montgomery Council (Book 1)

Watermelon Daiquiris

Pulp from a 2½-pound
  watermelon, seeded, cut
  into pieces and chilled
1 cup plus 2 tablespoons
  dark rum

½–⅔ cup fresh lime juice,
  or to taste
3 tablespoons superfine sugar
3 teaspoons orange-flavored
  liqueur

In a blender or food processor fitted with the steel blade, purée watermelon, rum, lime juice, sugar, and liqueur until mixture is smooth. Divide mixture among chilled, stemmed glasses. Makes 6 drinks.

Katherine Creamer, Mobile Council (Book 1)

Tropical Berry Blast Smoothie

1 banana, cut into quarters
1 (8-ounce) can crushed
   pineapple, drained

1 cup skim milk
½ cup frozen strawberries,
   thawed

Combine banana, pineapple, skim milk, and strawberries in a food processor container and process until smooth. Serve immediately in tall glasses. Yields 2 servings.

Gussie Evans, Mobile Council (Book 4)

Ruby's Party Cheese Ball

1 (8-ounce) package cream
   cheese, softened
12 ounces shredded sharp
   Cheddar cheese
½ cup chopped onion
½ cup chopped green bell
   pepper

1 tablespoon Worcestershire
2 teaspoons garlic salt
½ teaspoon cayenne pepper
1 cup chopped pecans

Beat cream cheese, Cheddar cheese, onion, green pepper, Worcestershire, garlic salt, and cayenne pepper in mixer bowl until combined. Shape into a ball; roll in pecans. Serve with assorted crackers. Yields 24 servings.

Ruby Webb, Mobile Council (Book 3)

Cheese Ball

2 (8-ounce) packages cream
  cheese, softened
¼ (8-ounce) can crushed
  pineapple, drained

¼ cup each: finely chopped bell
  pepper and onion
2 cups chopped pecans, divided
1 tablespoon seasoned salt

Whip cream cheese with fork until creamy. Add all ingredients except 1 cup pecans; mix and form into ball. Roll in remaining 1 cup pecans. Wrap in aluminum foil and let it set overnight in frig. (This is very important, so onion and bell pepper taste will not be so strong.)

Carol D. Adams, Mobile Council (Book 1)

Easy-As-Pie Sausage Balls

10 ounces shredded sharp
  Cheddar cheese
3 cups baking mix

1 pound hot or mild bulk
  sausage

Melt cheese in saucepan over low heat. Add baking mix and sausage; mix well. Shape into small balls and place on a baking sheet. Bake at 325° for 25 minutes. Yields 6 dozen.

Betty M. Jones-Moon, Birmingham Life Club (Book 4)

Pinwheel Chicken Roll-Ups

4 ounces light cream cheese,
  softened
2 tablespoons low-fat sour
  cream
1 tablespoon hot red pepper
  jelly
3 (9-inch) flour tortillas

1 cup chopped cooked chicken
½ cup chopped lettuce
½ cup shredded reduced-fat
  sharp Cheddar cheese
⅓ cup chopped green onions
⅓ cup chopped red bell pepper

Combine cream cheese, sour cream, and pepper jelly in a small bowl; mix well. Spread over tortillas. Combine chicken, lettuce, cheese, green onions, and bell pepper in a medium bowl; mix well. Sprinkle mixture over tortillas. Roll up tortillas to enclose filling.

Wrap individually in plastic wrap and chill 2 hours or longer. Cut off and discard ends of rolls; cut each roll into 8 or 9 slices. Yields 12 servings.

Debbie Morris, Birmingham South Cahaba Council (Book 4)

Olive Balls

1 (5-ounce) jar Old English
  cheese spread
1 stick margarine, softened

1 cup all-purpose flour
½ teaspoon red pepper
36 small pimento-stuffed olives

Combine cheese and margarine in a bowl and mix until smooth. Add flour and red pepper and mix to form a dough. Pinch off small amounts of dough and press flat in the hand. Place an olive in the center and shape dough to enclose olive completely. Place on a baking sheet and chill 3–4 hours. Bake at 375° for 15 minutes or until golden brown. You may freeze unbaked balls for up to 2 months. Yields 3 dozen.

Nelda Goodwin, Birmingham Life Club (Book 4)

Chili Cheese Fondue

1 pound hamburger, cooked,
  drained
1 pound American cheese,
  cut in small pieces
1 (4-ounce) can chopped green
  chiles

1 (10-ounce) can Ro-Tel
  tomatoes
1 teaspoon Worcestershire
½ teaspoon chili powder

Place all ingredients in slow cooker. Stir constantly until cheese melts; cook on HIGH for 1 hour. Serve with tortilla chips.

Jane Patterson, Riverchase Council (Book 1)

Herbed Cheese Spread

2 (8-ounce) packages cream
  cheese, softened
1 stick butter, softened
2 garlic cloves, minced
¼ teaspoon dried dill weed
¼ teaspoon dried basil
¼ teaspoon dried marjoram
¼ teaspoon dried thyme
¼ teaspoon dried oregano
¼ teaspoon salt
¼ teaspoon black pepper
Cayenne pepper to taste

Combine cream cheese, butter, garlic, dill weed, basil, marjoram, thyme, oregano, salt, black pepper, and cayenne pepper in a mixing bowl or food processor container and mix until smooth. Spoon into a serving crock or bowl. Serve with crackers. Store in refrigerator for up to 3 weeks or in freezer for up to 1 month. Yields 10–12 servings.

Frankie Vaughn, Selma Life Club (Book 4)

Charleston Cheese

1 (8-ounce) package cream
  cheese, softened
1 cup shredded sharp
  Cheddar cheese
½ cup mayonnaise
12 butter crackers, crushed
8 slices bacon, crisp-fried,
  crumbled, or real bacon bits

Combine cream cheese, Cheddar cheese, and mayonnaise in a bowl and mix well. Spoon into a greased quiche dish. Top with cracker crumbs. Bake at 350° for 15–20 minutes, or until heated through. Sprinkle with bacon and serve warm with crackers. Yields 15–20 servings.

Leigh Rice, Birmingham South Cahaba Council (Book 4)

Parmesan Party Dip

2 cups sour cream
1 cup shredded sharp Cheddar
  cheese
½ cup grated Parmesan cheese

4 slices bacon, cooked crispy,
  crumbled
¼ cup sliced green onions

Combine sour cream and cheeses; mix well. Stir in bacon and onions; chill. Garnish with additional green onions, if desired. Serve with vegetable dippers or chips.

Frances Crenshaw, Birmingham East Council (Book 1)

Cocktail Meatballs

2 pounds ground round
1 envelope onion soup mix
1 egg

1 teaspoon Worcestershire
½ cup bread crumbs

Mix together and form into balls. Put in refrigerator for at least ½ hour. Makes about 60 balls.

SAUCE:
1 (7-ounce) jar grape jelly
1 (10-ounce) bottle chili sauce

2 teaspoons lemon juice
½ cup water

Mix and simmer ½ hour; add uncooked meatballs and continue to simmer for ½ hour. If made a day ahead and warmed up, the flavor is much better.

Frances H. Lewis, Birmingham South Council (Book 2)

Sausage-Stuffed Mushrooms

12–15 large fresh mushrooms
2 tablespoons chopped onion
6 teaspoons butter or
   margarine, divided
1 tablespoon lemon juice
¼ teaspoon dried basil
Salt and pepper to taste

4 ounces bulk Italian sausage,
   browned
1 tablespoon chopped fresh
   parsley
2 tablespoons dry bread crumbs
2 tablespoons grated Parmesan
   cheese

Remove and chop mushroom stems, reserving the caps. Press chopped stems with paper towels to remove any moisture. In a skillet, sauté stems with onion in 4½ teaspoons butter until tender. Add lemon juice, basil, salt and pepper. Cook until most of the liquid has evaporated. Cool to room temperature. Add sausage and parsley. Spoon into mushroom caps. Mix bread crumbs and cheese in a bowl. Sprinkle over mushroom stuffing and dot with remaining 1½ teaspoons butter. Place in a greased baking pan. Bake at 400° for 20 minutes, basting occasionally with accumulated pan juices. Serve hot. Yields 12–15 servings.

Gail Hyatt, Anniston Council (Book 4)

Appetillas

1 package large tortillas
2 (8-ounce) packages cream
  cheese, softened
⅓ cup mayonnaise
¼–½ cup chopped green
  onions

¼ cup chopped black olives
¼ cup chopped green olives
¼ cup grated Parmesan cheese
2 (2½-ounce) packages thinly
  sliced cooked ham

Let tortillas stand at room temperature 15 minutes or longer. Combine cream cheese, mayonnaise, green onions, black olives, green olives, and Parmesan cheese in a bowl; mix well. Spread a thin layer over tortillas. Arrange ham over tortillas and roll up tortillas tightly to enclose filling. Wrap individually in plastic wrap and chill 3 hours or longer. Slice ¼-inch thick to serve. Yields 80 servings.

Susan Robinson, Birmingham Metro Council (Book 4)

Taco Dip

1 pound ground beef
2 (9-ounce) cans bean dip
2 cups sour cream
1 envelope taco seasoning mix
2 large tomatoes, chopped

4 green onions, chopped
2 (4-ounce) cans chopped black
  olives, drained
2 cups shredded Cheddar cheese

Brown ground beef in skillet, stirring until crumbly; drain. Spread bean dip on large platter. Sprinkle with ground beef. Spread with mixture of sour cream and seasoning mix. Sprinkle tomatoes, green onions, black olives, and cheese over top. Serve with taco-flavored tortilla chips. Yields 32 servings.

Jim Kiker, Birmingham Life Club (Book 3)

Crabmeat Mornay

1 stick butter
4 or 5 green onions, chopped
½ cup finely chopped fresh
   parsley
2 tablespoons all-purpose flour
1 pint half-and-half

½ pound grated Swiss cheese
1 tablespoon sherry
Red pepper to taste
Salt to taste
1 pound fresh lump crabmeat

Melt butter in heavy pot; sauté onions and parsley. Blend in flour, half-and-half, and cheese, stirring until cheese is melted. Add other ingredients and gently fold in crabmeat. Can be served in a chafing dish with Melba toast rounds or in pastry shells.

Anne Spragins, Birmingham East Council (Book 1)

Has any means of communication revolutionized the daily lives of ordinary people more than the telephone? Simply described, it is a system which converts sound, specifically the human voice, to electrical impulses of various frequencies and then back to a tone that sounds like the original voice.

Ham and Cheese Puffs

1 loaf thin white bread   **Butter, softened**

Trim crust from bread; cut each slice into 4 squares. Toast squares on one side. Turn over and spread thin layer of butter on each square before applying mixtures.

HAM MIXTURE:

1 cup canned deviled ham   **¼ cup mayonnaise**
2 teaspoons prepared mustard   **1 teaspoon finely grated onion**
½ teaspoon Worcestershire   **1 teaspoon baking powder**

Combine all ingredients; mix well.

CHEESE MIXTURE:

¾ cup grated Cheddar cheese   **1 teaspoon grated onion**
1 egg, beaten   **1 teaspoon baking powder**

Combine all ingredients; mix well.

Spread Ham Mixture to edges of each bread square; top with Cheese Mixture. At this point, puffs may be frozen. When ready to serve, remove from freezer and place under broiler until topping puffs and is brown. Serve at once. Puffs should not be removed from freezer until ready to broil. Do not allow to thaw.

Elsie Hard, Riverchase Council (Book 1)

Ham and Cheese Sandwiches

SAUCE:

1 stick margarine

2 tablespoons sugar

1 tablespoon grated onion

2 tablespoons poppy seeds

2 tablespoons mustard

Salt and pepper to taste

Combine ingredients in saucepan; bring to a boil. Remove from heat; set aside.

2 packages small dinner rolls

1½ pounds deli ham

1 package Swiss cheese slices

Cut rolls in halves; brush with Sauce on both sides. Layer ham and cheese on bottom halves of rolls; put top halves back on. Brush with remaining Sauce. Cover with foil. Bake at 300° for 15 minutes or until cheese melts.

Louise Blanton, Birmingham Life Member Club (Book 2)

Carrot Sandwiches

2 (8-ounce) packages cream
  cheese, softened

4 small carrots, grated

1 tablespoon onion juice

Salt and pepper to taste

Mayonnaise to moisten

½ cup chopped pecans

Brown sandwich bread

In mixer, cream cheese, carrots, onion juice, salt, pepper, and enough mayonnaise to moisten. Add pecans. Trim bread; spread with filling and roll like jellyroll. Chill or freeze before slicing. Freezes well.

Beverly Hearn, Riverchase Council (Book 1)

Blue Cheese Cookies

6 ounces sharp Cheddar cheese
3 ounces blue cheese
½ pound margarine, softened
2¾ cups all-purpose flour
1 cup chopped pecans
1 tablespoon Worcestershire

½ teaspoon garlic salt
½ teaspoon celery salt
½ teaspoon paprika
½ teaspoon salt
Dash of cayenne pepper

Grate Cheddar cheese and mix with blue cheese; add all other ingredients and mix well. Shape into a log; wrap in wax paper. Refrigerate to chill. Slice thin; bake at 375° for 10 minutes or till slightly browned.

Eileen Bevis, Tri-Cities Council (Book 2)

Peach Mango Guacamole

2 avocados
Juice of ½ lemon
1 large peach, chopped
½ mango, chopped

½ cup chopped pineapple
¾ cup salsa

Mash avocados in a bowl and add lemon juice; mix well. Add peach, mango, and pineapple; mix well. Stir in salsa. Serve with chips. Yields 8–10 servings.

Elaine Hyatt, Gadsden Life Club (Book 4)

Mother's Party Mix

3 (16-ounce) packages Chex
  cereal
1 (16-ounce) package pretzels
6 cups pecans
2 cups margarine

½ cup Worcestershire
1 (2-ounce) bottle Tabasco
¼ cup garlic powder
Salt to taste

Combine cereal, pretzels, and pecans in 3 large baking pans; mix well. Combine margarine, Worcestershire, Tabasco, garlic powder, and salt in saucepan; mix well. Cook until margarine melts, stirring constantly. Pour over cereal mixture, tossing to coat. Bake at 250° for 1 hour, stirring every 10 minutes. Cool for 1 hour. Store in airtight container. Yields 100 servings.

Note: Remove pretzels by hand from package in order to prevent excess salt combining with mixture

Mary Ann Hallmark, Birmingham South Council (Book 3)

Coated Pecans

2 cups pecan halves
1 cup sugar
5 tablespoons water

⅛–¼ teaspoon salt
1½ teaspoons vanilla
1½ teaspoons cinnamon

Roast pecans 10–12 minutes at 300°. In large saucepan combine remaining ingredients; cook on high approximately 2 minutes or until a soft-ball forms in water. Remove from heat; add pecans and stir by hand until coated. Pour out on wax paper and separate.

Jeanne Anderson, Montgomery Council (Book 1)

Bread and Breakfast

1878
Butterstamp

The first telephone with a combined receiver-transmitter that could be held in the hand looked like a butterstamp—hence its name. You talked into one end, turned the instrument around, and listened to the other end. The push button signaled the operator. This model was in service when the world's first commercial switchboard opened in New Haven, Connecticut, in 1878. Western Union opened the first large city exchange in San Francisco that same year. The public switched telephone network was born; no longer limited to people on the same wire, folks could now talk to many others on different lines.

Low-Fat Buttermilk Cornbread

2 cups self-rising cornmeal   1½ cups buttermilk
2 tablespoons vegetable oil   1 egg

Combine cornmeal, oil, buttermilk, and egg in bowl; mix well.
Pour a small amount of additional oil into cast-iron skillet. Preheat
skillet in 450° oven. Sprinkle a small amount of cornmeal over bottom of skillet. Pour in cornmeal batter. Bake at 450°–500° for 15–20
minutes or until golden brown. Yields 8 servings.

Melda H. Hicks, Anniston Council (Book 3)

Okra Cornbread

½ cup hush puppy mix   1 egg, beaten
½ teaspoon Cajun seasoning   ½ cup milk
1 (8-ounce) can cream-style   3 tablespoons vegetable oil
  corn   2 cups thinly sliced okra

Combine hush puppy mix and Cajun seasoning in a mixing bowl;
mix well. Add corn, egg, milk, and oil; mix well. Stir in okra. Pour
into a greased 8-inch-square baking pan. Bake at 350° for 45 minutes. Cut into squares. Yields 9 servings.

Hazel Campbell, Birmingham Life Club (Book 4)

Clyde's Broccoli Cornbread

2 (7-ounce) packages cornbread mix
¼ cup butter, softened
4 eggs, lightly beaten
12 ounces small-curd cottage cheese
1 (10-ounce) package frozen chopped broccoli, thawed

Combine cornbread mix, butter, eggs, and cottage cheese in bowl; mix well. Drain broccoli; stir into batter. Spoon into lightly greased 9x13-inch baking pan. Bake at 350° for 30 minutes or until golden brown. Cool slightly before cutting. Serve warm or cool. Store leftovers in refrigerator. Yields 15 servings.

Helen Shirley, Birmingham Life Club (Book 3)

Mexican Cornbread

2 (6-ounce) packages corn muffin mix
1 large onion, chopped
1 (16-ounce) can cream-style corn
½ cup corn oil
3 eggs, beaten
2 cups milk
3 tablespoons chopped jalapeño peppers
1 tablespoon jalapeño pepper liquid

Combine corn muffin mix, onion, corn, corn oil, eggs, milk, and jalapeño peppers and liquid in bowl; mix well. Pour into greased 9x13-inch baking pan. Bake at 310° for 1½ hours or until golden brown. Let stand for 1½ hours before serving. Yields 15 servings.

Glendora James, Decatur Council (Book 3)

Jalapeño Cornbread

3 cups self-rising cornmeal
3 cups grated cheese
3 eggs, beaten
2½ cups sweet milk
1 large onion, chopped very
   fine

1 (15-ounce) can cream-style
   corn
½ cup cooking oil
½ cup jalapeño pepper, cut
   fine
8 slices bacon, cooked, crumbled

Combine all together except bacon. Mix very well. Add bacon; mix well. Bake 45 minutes at 350° in big pan or 2 black cast-iron skillets.

Doris Holder, Decatur Council (Book 2)

Anne's Biscuits

2 cups self-rising flour
1 teaspoon baking powder
¼ teaspoon baking soda

¼ cup shortening
¾ cup buttermilk

Combine flour, baking powder, and baking soda in a mixing bowl; mix well. Cut shortening in with a pastry blender until mixture is crumbly. Add buttermilk and stir with a spoon until well mixed (the dough will be moist). Turn onto a lightly floured surface and kneed lightly several times, adding a small amount of flour as necessary. Roll dough to desired thickness. Cut into biscuits using a 2-inch biscuit cutter. Arrange biscuits on a lightly greased baking sheet. Bake at 500° until brown. Yields 8–12 biscuits.

Imogene Davis, Birmingham Life Club (Book 4)

Angel Biscuits

1 package dry yeast
¼ cup warm water
2½ cups all-purpose flour
½ teaspoon baking soda
1 teaspoon baking powder

1 teaspoon salt
2 tablespoons sugar
½ cup shortening
1 cup buttermilk

Dissolve yeast in warm water. Mix dry ingredients. Cut in shortening as for biscuit dough. Add buttermilk and yeast mixture; blend thoroughly. Turn dough out onto a floured cloth and knead as for regular biscuits. Roll out and cut biscuits. Place biscuits in a greased pan. Let dough rise for a few minutes before baking 12–15 minutes at 400°.

Virginia H. Greene, Birmingham Central Council (Book 1)

Cinnamon Biscuits

2 cups biscuit mix
½ cup brown sugar

2 teaspoons cinnamon
⅔ cup milk

Mix biscuit mix, brown sugar, and cinnamon in mixing bowl; add milk. Drop by tablespoon onto greased pan; bake at 400° for 10–15 minutes.

TOPPING:

¾ cup powdered sugar
1 teaspoon vanilla

3 teaspoons milk
Nuts and raisins (optional)

Mix ingredients well; spread on top of biscuits while hot. Nuts and raisins may be added to biscuits, if desired.

Mrs. Jack E. Gentte, Sr., Montgomery Council (Book 1)

Buttermilk Biscuits

1 cup self-rising flour	½ cup buttermilk
1 teaspoon sugar	1–2 tablespoons margarine,
¼ cup shortening	softened

Sift flour into bowl. Add sugar. Cut in shortening until crumbly. Add buttermilk; mix well. Roll or pat to ½-inch thickness on floured surface. Cut with biscuit cutter. Arrange on greased baking sheet. Brush with margarine. Let stand 5–10 minutes. Bake at 450° for 10 minutes or until golden brown. Serve hot. Yields 7 servings.

Variations: Cheese Biscuits: Add ⅓ cup shredded sharp cheese. Drop by spoonfuls onto baking sheet. Brush with butter; sprinkle with garlic powder and bake.

Yeast Biscuits: Increase sugar to 2 teaspoons; add ½ envelope dry yeast to flour mixture. Heat buttermilk to slightly warmer than room temperature before adding. Let stand 10–20 minutes before baking.

Maxine Pinckard (Mrs. Ken Pinckard), Montgomery Council
(Book 3)

One-Rise Cheesy Onion Bread

1 (16-ounce) package hot roll
  mix
⅔ cup very warm water
  (105°–115°)
¼ cup butter or margarine,
  softened

¼ cup cornmeal
1 tablespoon instant minced
  onion
1 egg

Generously grease 1½-quart round casserole or 5x9-inch loaf pan; sprinkle lightly with cornmeal. In a large bowl, dissolve yeast from hot mix in warm water. Stir in butter. Add cornmeal, onion, and egg; blend well. Add hot roll mix; blend well.

On floured surface, knead about 15 strokes. Shape into a ball or loaf. Place in a greased pan. Cover; let rise in warm place until light and doubled in size, 30–45 minutes. Preheat oven to 375°.

TOPPING:

½ cup shredded Cheddar
  cheese
1 tablespoon cornmeal
½ teaspoon instant minced
  onion

½ teaspoon poppy or sesame
  seeds
2 tablespoons milk
1 egg

Combine Topping ingredients; spoon over bread. Bake 30–35 minutes or until golden brown. Loaf may be covered with foil last 10 minutes to avoid overbrowning. Loosen edges; immediately remove from pan. Makes 1 loaf.

Note: High altitude—5200 feet; bake at 375° for 40–45 minutes.

Elaine Shelton, Huntsville Council (Book 2)

Quick Rolls

2 cups self-rising flour   1 teaspoon sugar
1 cup milk   4 teaspoons mayonnaise

Grease and flour 12 muffin cups and set aside. Combine flour, milk, sugar, and mayonnaise in a mixing bowl and beat until blended. Fill prepared muffin cups ⅔ full. Bake at 400° for 15 minutes or until golden brown. For 12 small rolls, reduce each ingredient by half and bake in small muffin cups. Yields 12 large rolls.

Kathryn Morgan, Gadsden Life Club (Book 4)

Sixty-Minute Rolls

1 envelope yeast   ⅓ cup melted shortening
⅓ cup warm water   1 cup buttermilk, at room
3 cups self-rising flour   temperature
1 tablespoon sugar   ¼ cup butter, melted

Dissolve yeast in warm water. Combine flour and sugar in bowl. Add shortening; mix until crumbly. Add yeast mixture and buttermilk; mix well. Knead on floured surface until smooth and elastic. Shape into rolls by rolling on floured surface and cutting as desired, or pinch off portions of dough and shape into biscuits. Roll in butter; arrange in greased baking pan. Let rise 60 minutes. Brush with remaining melted butter. Bake at 450° until golden brown. Yields 16 servings.

Carolyn Brouillette, Anniston Council (Book 3)

Thirty-Minute Rolls

3 cups (about) self-rising flour
½ cup sugar
1 envelope dry yeast

1½ cups water
½ cup shortening
1 egg

Mix 3 cups flour, sugar, and dry yeast in a large mixing bowl. Heat water and shortening in a saucepan to 225° or until shortening melts. Stir into flour mixture. Add egg and mix well. Add enough remaining flour to make a stiff dough. Turn dough onto a lightly floured surface, roll, and cut into rolls. Arrange rolls on a greased baking sheet. Let rise 30 minutes. Bake at 400° until brown. Yields 1½ dozen.

Imogene Davis, Birmingham Life Club (Book 4)

Quick Low-Fat Monkey Bread

1 cup sugar
1 tablespoon cinnamon
2 (16-ounce) loaves frozen bread
  dough, thawed

6 tablespoons margarine, melted

Mix sugar and cinnamon in bowl. Slice each loaf into 14 thin slices. Cut or tear each slice into 10–12 small pieces. Dip dough pieces into melted margarine; roll in cinnamon-sugar to coat. Place pieces in Bundt pan or 2 loaf pans. Preheat oven to 180°; turn off oven. Place baking pans in warm oven. Let rise for 2 hours. Bake at 375° for 20 minutes or until golden brown. Invert onto serving plate. Pull off pieces to eat with your fingers like a monkey. Yields 16 servings.

Eileen Knapp, Bon Secour Life Club (Book 3)

Pear Bread

1½ cups sugar
1½ cups corn oil
3 eggs
1 teaspoon vanilla extract
3 cups sifted all-purpose flour
1½ teaspoons baking soda

1 teaspoon salt
1 teaspoon cinnamon
1 teaspoon nutmeg
½ teaspoon ground cloves
3 cups finely chopped peeled
   fresh pears

Combine sugar, corn oil, eggs, and vanilla in a mixing bowl and beat until well blended. Mix flour, baking soda, salt, cinnamon, nutmeg, and cloves together. Add to sugar mixture gradually, beating well after each addition. Add pears and stir until well mixed. Pour batter into 2 greased and floured loaf pans. Bake at 350° for 45–55 minutes or until loaves test done; do not overbake. Cool in pans for several minutes. Turn onto wire racks to cool. You may substitute apples for pears. Yields 2 loaves.

Barbara Odom Horton, Mobile Council (Book 4)

Apple-Walnut Bread

2 cups sugar
1 cup vegetable oil
3 eggs
2 teaspoons vanilla extract
3 cups all-purpose flour

1 teaspoon salt
1 teaspoon cinnamon
1 teaspoon baking soda
3 cups chopped apples
1 cup chopped walnuts

Combine sugar, oil, eggs, and vanilla in bowl; mix well. Sift in dry ingredients; mix well. Stir in apples and walnuts. Pour into 2 greased and floured 5x9-inch loaf pans. Sprinkle with a small amount of additional sugar. Bake at 350° for 1 hour or until loaves test done. Remove from pans to cool on wire racks. Yields 24 servings.

Gertrude Patterson, Birmingham Life Club (Book 3)

Apricot Quick Bread

1 cup dried apricots
1 cup sugar
2 tablespoons butter, softened
1 egg
2 cups all-purpose flour
2 teaspoons baking powder

1 teaspoon salt
¼ teaspoon baking soda
½ cup orange juice
½ cup water
½ cup chopped walnuts
   (optional)

Soak apricots in warm water to cover 30 minutes. Drain apricots; cut into quarters; set aside. Combine sugar, butter, and egg in a mixing bowl and beat until light and fluffy. Combine flour, baking powder, salt, and baking soda; mix well. Combine orange juice and water. Add flour mixture and orange juice to sugar mixture alternately, mixing well after each addition. Stir in apricots and walnuts. Pour into a greased loaf pan. Let stand 20 minutes. Bake at 350° for 1 hour or until a knife inserted in center comes out clean. Cool in pan several minutes. Turn onto a wire rack to cool completely. Yields 1 loaf.

Francis Tucker, Selma Life Club (Book 4)

Blueberry Muffins

2 cups all-purpose flour
1 cup sugar
2 teaspoons baking powder
½ teaspoon salt
½ cup butter

½ cup milk
2 eggs, beaten
1 teaspoon vanilla
2½ cups blueberries, divided
Sugar for top of muffins

Preheat oven to 375°. Grease and flour muffin tins. Mix dry ingredients; cut in butter. Combine milk, eggs, and vanilla. Add moist ingredients all at once and stir just until moistened. Crush ½ cup blueberries and add to mixture. Fold in remaining 2 cups whole berries. Put in muffin tins and sprinkle with sugar. Bake 35 minutes. Makes 12 muffins.

Pat Gary (Book 2)

Orange Muffins

1 stick butter, softened
¾ cup sugar
2 eggs
1 teaspoon baking soda
1 cup buttermilk

2 cups all-purpose flour
½ teaspoon salt
1 cup raisins
Zest of 1 orange

Cream butter and sugar in a large mixing bowl until light and fluffy. Add eggs and beat well. Dissolve baking soda in buttermilk. Sift flour and salt together. Add flour mixture to creamed mixture alternately with buttermilk mixture, mixing well after each addition. Process raisins and orange zest in food processor until finely chopped. Add to muffin batter; mix well. Spoon batter into 12 greased muffin cups. Bake at 400° for 20 minutes or until golden brown. Yields 1 dozen.

Hazel Campbell, Birmingham Life Club (Book 4)

Cinnamon Bran Muffins

3 cups bran cereal (raisin or
  whole bran)
1 cup boiling water
2½ cups all-purpose flour
¾ cup sugar
2½ teaspoons baking soda

1½ teaspoons cinnamon
½ teaspoon salt
2 eggs
2 cups buttermilk
½ cup oil
½ cup currants or raisins

In large bowl, stir cereal with water; moisten evenly. Set aside to cool. Stir together flour, sugar, baking soda, cinnamon, and salt; set aside. Stir eggs, buttermilk, oil, and currants into cereal mixture until well blended; stir in flour mixture until well blended. Bake or store for future.

Before using, stir to distribute currants. Fill lightly greased muffin cups ⅔–¾ full. Bake in preheated 425° oven 20 minutes or until tops spring back. Makes 24–30.

Note: Batter will keep in airtight container, in refrigerator, approximately 4 weeks.

Shirley DuPont, Birmingham South Council (Book 1)

Butter Pecan Muffins

1½ cups self-rising flour
1 cup chopped pecans
½ cup packed brown sugar
1 egg, beaten

¾ cup milk
½ cup butter, melted
½ teaspoon vanilla extract

Combine flour, pecans, and brown sugar in large bowl; mix well. Beat egg with milk, butter, and vanilla in medium bowl. Add to pecan mixture; stir just until mixed. Fill greased muffin cups ⅔ full. Bake at 400° for 15–18 minutes or until golden brown. Yields 12 servings.

Nancy Morgan, Decatur Council (Book 3)

Pecan Pie Mini-Muffins

1 cup packed brown sugar
½ cup all-purpose flour
1 cup chopped pecans

2 eggs, beaten
⅔ cup butter, melted

Combine brown sugar, flour, and pecans in a mixing bowl. Blend eggs and butter in a small bowl. Add to pecan mixture; mix well. Fill greased miniature muffin cups ⅔ full. Bake at 350° for 20–25 minutes, or until golden brown and muffins test done. Remove from muffin cups immediately. Cool on wire racks. Yields 2½ dozen.

Linda McAdams, Shoals Life Club (Book 4)

Coffee Cake

1½ sticks margarine, softened
1 cup sugar
2 eggs
1 cup sour cream
2 cups all-purpose flour

1 teaspoon baking powder
1 teaspoon baking soda
½ teaspoon salt
1 teaspoon nutmeg

Cream margarine and sugar in a mixing bowl until light and fluffy. Add eggs and sour cream and beat until smooth. Sift flour, baking powder, baking soda, salt, and nutmeg together. Add to sour cream mixture and beat until well blended. Pour batter into greased and floured cake pan. Sprinkle Topping evenly over batter. Refrigerate, covered, overnight.

Bake, uncovered, at 325° for 40–45 minutes or until golden brown. Yields 5–8 servings.

TOPPING:
¾ cup packed brown sugar
1 teaspoon cinnamon

¾ cup chopped pecans

Mix brown sugar and cinnamon in a small bowl. Add pecans and stir until well mixed. Yields 1½ cups.

Mary Alice Neal, Birmingham Life Club (Book 4)

Nutty Orange Coffee Cake

1 cup sugar
¾ cup finely chopped pecans
1 tablespoon grated orange zest
2 (11-ounce) cans buttermilk
  biscuits

4 ounces reduced-fat cream
  cheese, softened
1 stick butter, melted

Combine sugar, pecans, and orange zest in a medium bowl; mix well; set aside. Separate biscuits. Place about ¾ teaspoon cream cheese in center of each, fold over to enclose cream cheese, and press edges together to seal. Lightly grease a 12-cup Bundt pan. Roll each filled biscuit in melted butter and then in pecan mixture to coat. Arrange biscuits with curved side down in grooves of Bundt pan; do not stack. Arrange any remaining biscuits around center of pan, filling in spaces. Drizzle any remaining butter over biscuits, and sprinkle with any remaining pecan mixture. Bake at 350° for 35–40 minutes or until golden brown. Invert coffee cake onto a serving plate. Drizzle Glaze over coffee cake and serve immediately. Yields 10–12 servings.

GLAZE:

1½ cups confectioners' sugar   2 tablespoons fresh orange juice

Sift confectioners' sugar into a small bowl. Add orange juice and blend well. Yields 1½ cups.

Chris Elsen, Gadsden Life Club (Book 4)

Date Coffee Cake

⅓ cup mashed banana
1 stick butter, softened
3 eggs
1 teaspoon vanilla extract
3 cups unbleached all-purpose
   flour

2 teaspoons baking powder
1 teaspoon baking soda
1½ cups water
1½ cups chopped dates

Combine banana and butter in a mixing bowl, and beat until smooth and creamy. Add eggs 1 at a time, beating after each addition. Beat in vanilla. Combine flour, baking powder, and baking soda; mix well. Reserve a small amount of flour mixture to mix with dates. Add remaining flour mixture and water alternately to banana mixture, mixing well after each addition. Toss reserved flour mixture with dates until coated. Stir coated dates into batter. Spread batter evenly in a greased and floured 9x13-inch cake pan. Sprinkle with Topping. Bake at 350° for 20–25 minutes or until a knife inserted in center comes out clean. Cool in pan on wire rack. Yields 8–10 servings.

TOPPING:

⅓ cup chopped dates
⅓ cup chopped walnuts

⅓ cup flaked coconut

Combine dates, walnuts, and coconut in a bowl; mix well. Yields 1 cup.

Louise Morrison, Tuscaloosa Council (Book 4)

Baked French Toast

8 (1½-inch) slices French
  bread
8 eggs
3 cups milk

1 teaspoon sugar
¾ teaspoon salt
1 tablespoon vanilla extract
2 tablespoons butter

Arrange bread slices in greased 9x13-inch baking dish. Beat eggs in medium bowl. Add milk, sugar, salt, and vanilla; beat until well mixed. Pour over bread. Refrigerate, covered with foil, overnight, or up to 36 hours.

Uncover; dot with butter. Bake, uncovered, at 350° for 45–50 minutes or until golden brown. Yields 4 servings.

Martha Bryan, Huntsville Life Club (Book 3)

Club Soda Pancakes

2 cups biscuit mix
½ cup vegetable oil

1 egg, beaten
1¼ cups club soda

Combine biscuit mix, oil, and egg in a mixing bowl. Add club soda; mix well. Ladle desired amount of batter onto a hot greased griddle. Bake until bubbly around edge, turn pancake over and bake until golden brown on both sides. Yields 1 dozen.

Narice Sutton, Birmingham Life Club (Book 4)

Sausage, Egg, and Cheese Quiche

1 pound bulk sausage
1 large yellow onion, chopped
1 green bell pepper, chopped
6 eggs

2 cups shredded extra sharp
   Cheddar cheese
2 All-Ready Pie Pastries

Brown sausage with onion and bell pepper in a skillet, stirring until sausage is crumbly; drain. Add eggs and cheese; mix well. Fit one of the pastries into a (9-inch) pie plate. Spoon sausage mixture into pastry-lined pie plate. Top with remaining pastry, sealing edge and cutting vents. Bake at 350° for 45–55 minutes or until set. Yields 6 servings.

Mary Ann Stanley, Mobile Council (Book 4)

Breakfast Casserole

6 slices bread, dried or toasted,
   cubed
1 pound hot bulk sausage
1½ cups shredded sharp
   Cheddar cheese

6 eggs
2 cups milk
1 teaspoon dry mustard
Salt and pepper to taste

Sprinkle bread cubes into greased 7x12-inch baking dish. Sprinkle sausage and cheese over bread. Beat eggs in mixer bowl. Add milk, dry mustard, salt and pepper; mix well. Pour over layers. Chill, covered with foil, overnight.

Bake, uncovered, at 350° for 40–45 minutes or until set and golden brown. Yields 8 servings.

Martha Bryan, Huntsville Life Club (Book 3)

Cheese Grits

2½ cups milk
¾ cup regular grits
½ cup margarine
½ teaspoon salt

⅓ cup grated Parmesan cheese
1 (5-ounce) jar sharp process
    cheese spread

Bring milk to a boil; add grits and cook until thickened, about 10 minutes, stirring often. Stir in margarine, salt, and cheese; spoon into lightly greased 1-quart casserole dish and bake at 325° for 20 minutes. Serves 6–8.

Gloria H. Ramage, Birmingham South Council (Book 1)

Garlic Grits Casserole

1 cup grits
4 cups water
1 teaspoon salt
1 stick margarine, cubed

1 (6-ounce) roll Kraft Garlic
    Cheese, cubed
2 eggs, beaten

Cook grits in water and salt. Add margarine and cheese; stir to dissolve. Add small amount of mixture to eggs. Return mixture to grits; stir to mix. Pour into buttered casserole dish. Bake at 350° until brown, about 1 hour.

Bonnie Mayfield, Anniston Council (Book 1)

Grits and Sausage Casserole

4 cups water
1 cup quick-cooking grits
1 teaspoon salt
1 stick margarine
1 pound bulk pork sausage

4 eggs, beaten
½ cup milk
1½ cups shredded Cheddar
   cheese, divided

Place water in a saucepan and bring to a boil. Add grits, stirring constantly. Stir in salt. Simmer 5 minutes. Remove from heat. Add margarine to hot mixture, stirring until melted. Brown sausage in a skillet, stirring until crumbly; drain. Whisk eggs and milk together in a bowl. Add sausage and egg mixture to grits; mix well. Stir in 1 cup cheese. Spoon into a 9x13-inch baking dish. Sprinkle remaining ½ cup cheese over top. Bake at 350° for 40 minutes or until set and bubbly. Yields 8–10 servings.

Emogene Husby, Mobile Council (Book 4)

Pear Marmalade

8 cups peeled, grated pears
6 cups sugar
1 lemon, thinly sliced

1 (6-ounce) can crushed
   pineapple

Combine pears, sugar, and lemon slices in saucepan; mix well. Cook 1½ hours or until very tender, stirring frequently. Stir in crushed pineapple. Cook 10 minutes longer. Spoon into sterilized jars, leaving ½ inch of head space; seal with 2-piece lids. Yields 80 servings.

Hazel Campbell, Birmingham Life Club (Book 3)

Karmen's Breakfast Pizza

1 pound bulk pork sausage
1 (8-count) package crescent
  rolls
3 eggs
¼ cup milk
½ teaspoon salt
⅛ teaspoon pepper

1 cup frozen hash brown
  potatoes, thawed
1 cup shredded sharp Cheddar
  cheese
2 tablespoons grated Parmesan
  cheese

Brown sausage in a skillet, stirring until crumbly; drain. Separate crescent roll dough into triangles. Arrange dough over bottom of a 12-inch pizza pan, pressing up the side of the pan and pressing perforations to seal. Combine eggs, milk, salt, and pepper in a bowl; mix well. Layer sausage, potatoes, Cheddar cheese, and egg mixture over the dough. Sprinkle Parmesan cheese over top. Bake at 375° for 25–30 minutes or until set. Yields 6 servings.

Karmen Patterson-Sutton, Birmingham Life Club (Book 4)

Soups, Stews, and Chilies

1882
Three-Box

This oak-encased instrument was the standard for many years and one of the first to place the crank more conveniently on the side. The top box contained a ringer and a switchhook. The middle box was a Blake transmitter, which was known for its improved voice clarity. The bottom, a cover for a wet cell battery, doubled as a writing shelf. To place a call, you turned the crank to ring the operator, then picked up the receiver. The operator would then answer and connect you to the party you wished to call. To signal the operator to disconnect the call, you would hang up the receiver and turn the crank to produce a short ring. This was called "ringing off."

French Onion Potato Soup

6–8 potatoes, peeled, chopped
½ small onion, chopped
2 (10¾-ounce) cans cream
of chicken soup
2 soup cans milk

1 (8-ounce) container French
onion dip
Shredded cheese
Bacon bits

Combine potatoes and onion with water to cover in a saucepan. Cook until tender; drain well. Combine potatoes, onion, cream of chicken soup, milk, and onion dip in a saucepan and mix well. Cook over low heat until heated through. Ladle into bowls. Sprinkle with cheese and bacon bits.

Linda D. Jackson, Montgomery Council (Book 4)

Hearty Potato Soup

6 medium potatoes, peeled,
cut into cubes
6 ribs celery, chopped
2 carrots, chopped
2 quarts water
1 onion, chopped

6 tablespoons butter
6 tablespoons flour
1 teaspoon salt
½ teaspoon pepper
1½ cups milk

Combine potatoes, celery, carrots, and water in a large stockpot. Cook 20 minutes or until tender; drain well, reserving cooking liquid and vegetables separately. Sauté onion in butter in stockpot until tender. Stir in flour, salt, and pepper. Stir in milk gradually. Cook until thickened, stirring constantly. Stir in potato mixture gently. Stir in enough of the reserved cooking liquid gradually to make soup the desired consistency. Yields 8–10 servings.

Mauntez Mayer, Anniston Council (Book 4)

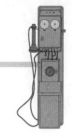

Cabbage Patch Soup

1 medium head cabbage,
  shredded
2 pounds ground chuck
1 large onion, chopped
1 large green bell pepper,
  chopped
Salt and pepper to taste

2 tablespoons sugar
2 (16-ounce) cans dark kidney
  beans
1 (14½-ounce) can stewed
  tomatoes
1 (6-ounce) can tomato paste
1 (10-ounce) can Ro-Tel tomatoes

Boil cabbage in water to cover in large stockpot for 5 minutes. Brown meat in skillet; drain. Add onion, bell pepper, salt and pepper. Combine all ingredients in stockpot and simmer for several hours. Leftovers freeze well.

Mike McDaniel, Riverchase Council (Book 2)

Spicy Cabbage Beef Soup

1 pound lean ground beef
1 large onion, chopped
5 cups chopped cabbage
2 (16-ounce) cans Mexican-
  style beans or kidney beans

3 (8-ounce) cans tomato sauce
4 beef bouillon cubes
1½ teaspoons cumin
½ teaspoon salt

Brown ground beef with onion in a Dutch oven or large saucepan, stirring frequently until ground beef is crumbly; drain well. Add cabbage, beans, tomato sauce, bouillon cubes, cumin, and salt; mix well. Bring to a boil; reduce heat. Simmer, covered, 5–6 hours. Yields 4–6 servings.

Anne Hancock, Gadsden Life Club (Book 4)

Quick-and-Easy Ground Beef Vegetable Soup

1 pound lean ground beef
1 (12-ounce) package frozen
  seasoning mix
1 (16-ounce) can cream-style
  corn
1 (10-ounce) can tomatoes with
  green chiles

1 (14½-ounce) can stewed
  tomatoes
1 (48-ounce) can vegetable juice
  cocktail
2 (15-ounce) cans mixed
  vegetables
1 (15-ounce) can Spanish rice

Brown ground beef in saucepan, stirring until crumbly; drain well. Add seasoning mix, corn, tomatoes with green chiles, stewed tomatoes, vegetable juice cocktail, mixed vegetables, and Spanish rice, and mix well. Bring to a boil; reduce heat. Simmer over low heat 30–40 minutes. Yields 4–6 servings.

Patricia V. Allen, Selma Life Club (Book 4)

Seven-Can Soup

1 pound ground chuck
1 (14½-ounce) can stewed
  tomatoes
1 (10-ounce) can tomatoes with
  green chiles
1 (10¾-ounce) can tomato soup
1 (15-ounce) can chili with
  beans

1 (10¾-ounce) can vegetable
  soup, or 1 (15-ounce) can
  mixed soup vegetables and 1
  bouillon cube
1 (15-ounce) can chili without
  beans
1 (15-ounce) can whole-kernel
  corn, or Mexicorn

Brown ground chuck in a saucepan, stirring until crumbly; drain well. Add stewed tomatoes, tomatoes with green chiles, tomato soup, chili with beans, vegetable soup, chili without beans, and corn; mix well. Cook until thickened, stirring occasionally. Yields 6–8 servings.

Anatalie Watson Fogg, Decatur Council (Book 4)

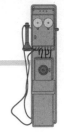

Cream of Tomato Soup

1 (28-ounce) can tomatoes
2 slices onion
1 bay leaf
1 teaspoon sugar
1 teaspoon salt

¼ teaspoon pepper
2 tablespoons butter or
  margarine
2 tablespoons all-purpose flour
1½ cups milk

Combine first 6 ingredients in a 2-quart saucepan. Simmer 10 minutes; sieve. Make a white sauce of butter, flour, and milk. Slowly add hot tomato mixture, stirring constantly. Serve at once. Serves 6.

Estelle Dean, Anniston Council (Book 2)

Santa Fe Soup

1 pound ground round
1 large onion, chopped
2 envelopes ranch salad
  dressing mix
2 envelopes taco seasoning mix
2 (11-ounce) cans shoepeg corn,
  drained
2 cups water
1 (15-ounce) can black beans

1 (15-ounce) can pinto beans
1 (15-ounce) can kidney beans
1 (14½-ounce) can whole
  tomatoes
1 (10-ounce) can tomatoes with
  green chiles
Shredded fat-free cheese
Fat-free sour cream
Chopped green onions

Brown ground round with onion in a Dutch oven, stirring frequently until ground round is crumbly; drain well. Add salad dressing mix, taco seasoning mix, corn, water, black beans, pinto beans, kidney beans, whole tomatoes, and tomatoes with green chiles; mix well. Bring to a boil; reduce heat. Simmer, covered, 2 hours. Ladle into bowls. Top each serving with cheese, sour cream, and green onions. Serve with tortillas or cornbread. Yields 8 servings.

Bertha Capps, Birmingham Life Club (Book 4)

Cream of Split Pea Soup

1 cup dried split peas
2 quarts cold water
1 small piece fat salt pork
½ small onion, quartered
4 tablespoons butter

3 tablespoons all-purpose flour
1¼ teaspoons salt
⅛ teaspoon pepper
2 cups milk

Pick over peas; cover with cold water and soak overnight; drain. Add cold water, pork, and onion. Simmer 4 hours, or until tender. Press through a sieve or potato ricer. Melt butter; add flour and stir to a smooth paste. Add pea pulp, salt, pepper, and milk. If too thick, add more milk. Makes 6–8 servings.

Faye Reid, Anniston Council (Book 2)

Squash Soup

3 pounds yellow squash
1 large onion, chopped
2 cloves garlic, minced
4 cups chicken broth (or 2 cans
   chicken soup and 2 cups
   water)

½ cup butter or margarine
½ cup vegetable oil
2 teaspoons salt
1 teaspoon white pepper
1 pint half-and-half

Cook squash, onion, and garlic in small amount of water until tender. Place in blender with small amount of chicken broth. Add other ingredients except half-and-half, including remaining chicken broth; stir until smooth. Refrigerate until ready to heat, then add half-and-half. Do not boil.

Mrs. R. E. Brinton, Birmingham East Council (Book 1)

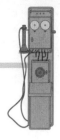

Yellow Chicken Soup

2–3 pounds chicken
3½ quarts water
2 medium onions, chopped
4 sticks celery, chopped
1 bay leaf
4 chicken bouillon cubes
3 tablespoons butter

½ cup rice
1 teaspoon red pepper
2 tablespoons turmeric
2 tablespoons chopped
   parsley
Salt and pepper to taste

Boil chicken pieces in water until tender and remove bone; add chicken back to water and cook 45 minutes. Add onions, celery, bay leaf, chicken cubes, butter, rice, and seasonings. Cook 45 minutes on low heat. Soup will be thick; add additional water for thinner soup.

Louise Berrey, Montgomery Council (Book 1)

Ham and Corn Chowder

2 cups diced cooked ham
1 cup chopped celery
½ cup chopped onion
½ cup butter or margarine,
   melted
3 (10-ounce) packages frozen
   cream-style corn, thawed

1 cup milk
½ teaspoon onion salt
½ teaspoon celery salt
½ teaspoon pepper
Fresh parsley, chopped
   (optional)

Sauté ham, celery, and onion in butter in a Dutch oven. Stir in remaining ingredients, except parsley, and bring to a boil. Reduce heat and simmer 20 minutes. Garnish with parsley, if desired. Yields about 6 cups.

Regina Cash, Anniston Council (Book 1)

Golden Cheese Chowder

1 cup butter or margarine	1 cup chopped celery
½ cup all-purpose flour	1 cup diced carrots
4 cups milk	½ cup diced onion
4 cups shredded sharp cheese	¾ teaspoon salt
3 cups water	¼ teaspoon pepper
4 medium potatoes, peeled, diced	2 cups diced, cooked ham
	Hot sauce to taste

Melt butter in a heavy 2-quart saucepan over low heat and add flour, stirring until smooth. Cook 1 minute; stir constantly. Gradually stir in milk; cook over medium heat, stirring constantly, until thick and bubbly. Add cheese, stirring until cheese is melted. Remove from heat and set aside. Combine water, vegetables, salt, and pepper in a 5-quart Dutch oven; heat to boiling. Reduce heat and cover; simmer 10 minutes or until vegetables are tender. Stir in all other ingredients. Cook over low heat until thoroughly heated; do not boil. Makes 12–14 servings.

Betty Floyd Parker, Montgomery Council (Book 1)

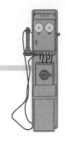

Hot Sausage Bean Chowder

1 pound hot bulk sausage
2 (16-ounce) cans red kidney beans
1 (14½-ounce) can tomatoes, broken up
1 quart water
1 large onion, chopped

1 bay leaf
1½ teaspoons seasoned salt
½ teaspoon garlic salt
½ teaspoon thyme
⅛ teaspoon pepper
3 or 4 potatoes, peeled, diced
2 (14-ounce) cans Niblets corn

In a large boiler, cook sausage until brown; drain well. Add remaining ingredients. Cover and cook at low temperature for about an hour.

Martha Pickrell, Birmingham South Council (Book 2)

Crab Bisque

1 cup chopped onion
1 cup chopped celery
3 tablespoons margarine
2 teaspoons salt
1 quart half-and-half

1 pound lump crabmeat
2 tablespoons parsley flakes
½ cup instant potato flakes
1 cup water

Sauté onion and celery in margarine in large Dutch oven. Add remaining ingredients, except potato flakes. Bring to a simmer. Add instant potato flakes. Stir till smooth.

Mary Jane Williams, Birmingham East Council (Book 2)

Delicious Beef Tip Crockpot Stew

1 pound beef tips, cut in
½-inch cubes
1 (14½-ounce) can sliced
stewed tomatoes and liquid
1 (14-ounce) can beef broth
1 large onion, chopped
2 potatoes, cut in ½-inch cubes
2 carrots, cut in ½-inch cubes
2 stalks celery, chopped

½ green bell pepper, chopped
⅛ teaspoon garlic powder
⅛ teaspoon minced garlic
⅛ teaspoon celery seed
⅛ teaspoon oregano
Adolph's meat tenderizer
1 tablespoon Worcestershire
¼ teaspoon Kitchen Bouquet

Put all ingredients in crockpot. Cook for 5–6 hours on LOW in crockpot, or longer if needed. Serve over split corn muffins.

Burt Knox, Birmingham Life Club (Book 2)

Chicken Brunswick Stew

2 broiling chickens, or 5
chicken breasts, boned
1 cup chicken broth
6 medium potatoes, peeled,
diced
4 medium onions, diced
1 cup ketchup

¼ cup soy sauce
½ cup barbeque sauce
2 (14½-ounce) cans stewed
tomatoes
1 (15-ounce) can lima beans
1 (12-ounce) can shoepeg corn
Salt and pepper to taste

Combine all ingredients in large stockpot. Cover and simmer for about 6 hours.

Gladys Lindsey, Montgomery Council (Book 2)

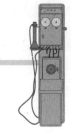

Oyster Stew

1 quart oysters
4 tablespoons chopped green
 onions
1 stick butter

1 teaspoon Worcestershire
1 quart milk, heated
Salt and pepper to taste

Drain oysters; reserve liquor. Sauté onions in butter until tender; remove onions. Heat oysters in remaining butter until edges curl. Combine all ingredients, including oyster liquor. Season to taste.

Note: For a richer stew, use ½ light cream and ½ milk.

Betty Parker, Montgomery Council (Book 1)

Chicken Gumbo

1 (3- to 4-pound) chicken
Salt and pepper to taste
4 cups water
¼ cup all-purpose flour
2 tablespoons oil
2½ cups chopped onions
3 stalks celery and tops

1½ cups chopped green bell
 peppers, divided
1 clove garlic, minced
1 (12-ounce) package little
 smoked sausage links, sliced
1 bunch green onions with tops

Simmer chicken, salt and pepper in water until tender. Remove chicken; debone and save broth. Brown flour in oil; add onions, celery, 1 cup peppers, garlic, and 2 cups chicken broth. Season with additional salt and pepper to taste. Simmer 1 hour. Add chicken and remaining broth; simmer 40 minutes. Add sliced sausage, green onions, and remaining ½ cup green peppers, Simmer 15 minutes. Serve over hot rice.

Leona Lathem, Riverchase Council (Book 2)

Okra Seafood Gumbo

Choctaw Indians' word for sassafras is "kombo," from which we get the word gumbo.

6 hard-shell crabs	1 cup diced cooked ham
2 pounds okra	1 (14½-ounce) can tomatoes
4 tablespoons bacon fat, divided	2 pounds raw shrimp, peeled
	6 cups water
2 tablespoons all-purpose flour	1 teaspoon salt
	Pinch of pepper
1 cup chopped onion	5 dashes Tabasco
½ cup chopped green onions	1 bay leaf
1 clove garlic, finely chopped	½ teaspoon thyme
1 green bell pepper, chopped	

Boil crabs until they turn red (about 20 minutes); set aside; reserve water. Wash okra and cut into ¼-inch rounds. Put 2 tablespoons bacon fat in iron skillet and fry okra, stirring often, to prevent burning, until it is browned and dried out, with all trace of sliminess gone.

In a deep pot, melt remaining 2 tablespoons bacon fat and blend in flour to make a roux, cooking and stirring until deep brown. Add chopped onion, green onions, garlic, and green pepper; stir and cook a few minutes, then add ham. Add tomatoes and raw shrimp. After cooking a few minutes, add cooked okra and 6 cups of crab-boiling water (or water). Add seasoning and let boil slowly about 2 hours, adding more water if necessary.

During this time, remove shell from crabs; crack claws with a nutcracker so they will pull apart easily, and either break bodies in halves, or remove meat from them, depending on which way you prefer to serve them. During the last half hour of cooking, add crab claws and halved bodies or meat to gumbo. Serve gumbo in a bowl over a mound of hot cooked rice. Serves 8.

Linda Unger, Riverchase Council (Book 1)

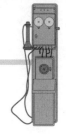

Chili

1 pound ground beef	1 (6-ounce) can tomato paste
1 pound ground chuck	1 teaspoon sugar
½ bell pepper, chopped	1 teaspoon salt
1 stalk celery, chopped	1 teaspoon pepper
1 small onion, chopped	1 teaspoon chili powder
1 (8-ounce) can tomato sauce	1 (15-ounce) can kidney beans

In large saucepan, brown meat; drain excess fat. Add bell pepper, celery, and onion; cook until tender. Add tomato sauce, tomato paste, sugar, salt, pepper, chili powder, and beans. Simmer about 30 minutes.

Rosemary Parker, Birmingham Central Council (Book 2)

Easy Chili

2 pounds ground beef	3–4 teaspoons chili powder
2 or 3 onions, chopped	¼ cup packed brown sugar
3 (14½-ounce) cans whole tomatoes	Salt and pepper to taste
1 (16-ounce) can chili beans	Garlic powder to taste

Brown ground beef with onions in large saucepan, stirring until ground beef is crumbly; drain. Add tomatoes, chili beans, chili powder, brown sugar, salt, pepper, and garlic powder; mix well. Simmer for 2 hours or until of desired consistency, stirring occasionally. Yields 8 servings.

Maxine Pinckard, Montgomery Council (Book 3)

Venison Chili

1 pound ground venison
½ pound ground chuck
1 (2¼-ounce) package Chili-O
  mix with onions
1 (14½-ounce) can stewed
  tomatoes

1 (15½-ounce) can Mexican-
  style beans
½ cup water
Shredded Cheddar cheese

Brown venison with ground chuck. Remove any excess fat. Add Chili-O mix. Mix well. Add tomatoes, beans, and water. Bring to a boil; reduce heat and simmer 10 minutes. Pour chili into bowls. Sprinkle with Cheddar cheese. Melt cheese in microwave or regular oven.

John Sumners, Birmingham South Council (Book 2)

$\mathcal{S}$alads

1892
Desk Set

The first common battery arrangement came into play in the 1890s, providing electricity to all telephones controlled by the central office. Previously, each customer's telephone needed its own battery to power the transmitter. The innovation of the common battery changed telephone design. The big, bulky wall sets with wet batteries providing power and cranks to signal the operator could now be replaced with sleek desk sets. Since the crank and batteries were no longer required, the subset could be mounted on the wall and out of the way. When you wanted to place a call, you would simply pick up the receiver and wait for the operator. When you finished your call, you could just hang up. Long-distance calling reached a major milestone in 1892, when telephone service between New York and Chicago began. This 950–mile circuit was the longest line possible with the existing technology.

Broccoli Salad
with Buttermilk Dressing

SALAD:

1 bunch broccoli
1 head cauliflower
1 small onion

1 cucumber
2 ribs celery
2 carrots

Chop broccoli, cauliflower, onion, cucumber, celery, and carrots. Combine vegetables in a salad bowl and mix well. Pour Buttermilk Dressing over the top. Toss to mix. Refrigerate, covered, until well chilled. Yields 8–10 servings.

BUTTERMILK DRESSING:

1 cup buttermilk
1 cup mayonnaise
¼ teaspoon onion salt

¼ teaspoon garlic salt
¼ teaspoon celery salt
⅛ teaspoon pepper

Combine buttermilk, mayonnaise, onion salt, garlic salt, celery salt, and pepper in a covered jar and shake well. Yields 2 cups.

Sara Cooley, Birmingham Life Club (Book 4)

Broccoli and Raisin Salad

1 cup mayonnaise
2 tablespoons vinegar
2 tablespoons sugar
2–3 stalks broccoli, chopped

1 cup raisins
1 medium red onion, chopped
4 or 5 slices bacon, crisp-fried,
    crumbled

Combine mayonnaise, vinegar, and sugar in large bowl; mix well. Add broccoli, raisins, onion, and bacon; mix well. Chill 30 minutes. Yields 8 servings.

Nina Green, Anniston Council (Book 3)

Marinated Vegetable Salad

1 (16-ounce) can cut green
  beans, drained
1 (16-ounce) can green peas,
  drained
1 (16-ounce) can whole-kernel
  corn, drained
2 cups chopped celery
½ cup chopped onion

1 (4-ounce) jar chopped
  pimentos, drained
1½ tablespoons salt
1 cup vinegar
½ cup oil
1 cup sugar
1 teaspoon paprika

Combine beans, peas, corn, celery, onion, pimentos, and salt in large bowl; mix gently. Chill for 1 hour; drain well. Add vinegar, oil, sugar, and paprika; mix gently. Chill, covered, several hours. May be stored in refrigerator for several days. Serve with a slotted spoon. Yields 12 servings.

Martha L. Bryan, Huntsville Life Club (Book 3)

Spinach Salad

¼ cup pine nuts
10 ounces fresh spinach,
  trimmed, torn
¾ cup thinly sliced dried
  apricots
3 tablespoons orange juice

1 teaspoon lemon juice
2 tablespoons oil
¾ teaspoon grated orange rind
Tabasco to taste
Salt to taste

Toast pine nuts in small skillet over medium heat for 4 minutes or until light brown. Combine with spinach and apricots in large glass bowl. Whisk orange juice, lemon juice, oil, orange rind, Tabasco, and salt together in small bowl. Add to salad; toss to coat well. Yields 8 servings.

Note: May substitute toasted slivered almonds for pine nuts.

Fran Rhodis, Mobile Life Club (Book 3)

Low-Fat German Potato Salad

5 slices bacon
¾ cup chopped onion
2 tablespoons flour
⅔ cup cider vinegar
1⅓ cups water

¼ cup sugar
1 teaspoon salt
¼ teaspoon pepper
6 cups sliced cooked potatoes
Boiled eggs (optional)

Fry bacon in large skillet until crisp. Remove and crumble bacon; drain skillet, reserving 3 tablespoons drippings. Sauté onion in reserved drippings in skillet until tender. Stir in flour. Add vinegar and water. Cook until slightly thickened, stirring constantly. Stir in sugar, salt, and pepper. Add potatoes and bacon; mix gently. Cook just until heated through. Serve warm. May add boiled eggs, if desired. Yields 8 servings.

Barbara Seegmiller, Life Member, Decatur Council (Book 3)

Hot German Potato Salad

10 medium potatoes, boiled
  in their skins
8 slices bacon, diced
2 medium onions, diced
¾ cup sugar
2 teaspoons dry mustard

2 eggs, beaten
¾ cup vinegar
Salt and pepper to taste
4 hard-boiled eggs, sliced
2 tablespoons chopped parsley

Peel and cube potatoes; put in an ovenware bowl or casserole. Fry bacon. Remove bacon from pan and reserve. Fry onions in bacon fat until tender, but not browned. Mix sugar and mustard together. Add to onions in frying pan; add beaten eggs and vinegar to onion mixture; cook until thickened, stirring constantly. Pour over potatoes; add salt and pepper to taste. Add reserved bacon and egg slices. Mix lightly. Heat in a 250° oven for 30 minutes or until ready to serve. Sprinkle parsley on top. Serves 8–10.

Joyce Reavis, Decatur Council (Book 1)

Perfect Potato Salad

5–8 pounds red potatoes,
  boiled, peeled
Salt to taste
12 eggs, hard-boiled

1 small onion, cut in wedges
1 quart Hellmann's mayonnaise
2 tablespoons black pepper

Chop potatoes coarsely, and place in a large bowl; sprinkle with salt. Combine eggs, onion, mayonnaise, and pepper in blender or food processor container. Process until smooth. Add to potatoes; mix well. Yields 10–12 servings.

Susan Neuhoff, Montgomery Council (Book 4)

Sour Cream Potato Salad

4 cups sliced, cooked potatoes
½ cup diced cucumber
1 onion, minced
¾ teaspoon celery seeds
1½ teaspoons salt
½ teaspoon pepper

3 hard-boiled eggs, separated
1½ cups sour cream
½ cup mayonnaise
¼ cup vinegar
1 teaspoon prepared mustard

Combine potatoes, cucumber, onion, celery seeds, salt, and pepper; blend carefully. Cut egg whites into small pieces and add to potato mixture. Mash yolks; add to sour cream, mayonnaise, vinegar and mustard; blend. Heat sour cream mixture slightly and pour over potatoes. Makes 8 servings.

Donna Campbell, Anniston Council (Book 2)

In 1877, Bell Telephone Company was formed to operate local telephone exchange operation, installing the first city exchange in Hartford, Connecticut.

Pitty Pat's Sweet Potato Salad

8 large sweet potatoes, peeled
1 (8-ounce) ¼-inch-thick ham
  slice
1 cup chopped green onions
1 cup chopped green bell
  pepper

1 cup spicy brown mustard
½ cup vegetable oil
1 tablespoon salt
1 tablespoon white pepper
1 tablespoon chopped fresh dill

Cut sweet potatoes into 2-inch strips. Steam 10–12 minutes or just until tender. Let stand until cool. Cut ham into ½-inch pieces. Combine sweet potatoes, ham, green onions, and bell pepper in a large bowl. Mix brown mustard, oil, salt, white pepper, and dill in a small bowl. Add to sweet potato mixture and mix well. Chill, covered, 2 hours or longer. Serve with pork chops or chicken. Yields 6 servings.

Alice Walski, Birmingham Life Club (Book 4)

Yummy Carrot Salad

4 or 5 large carrots, scraped,
  washed
1 (8-ounce) can crushed
  pineapple, drained

4 tablespoons sugar
½ cup raisins
⅓ cup mayonnaise

Grate carrots finely. Put into medium-size salad bowl, adding pineapple, sugar, raisins, and mayonnaise; toss well. Refrigerate until ready to serve.

Note: Bananas and apples may be added also.

Billie Bays, Decatur Council (Book 1)

Chicken Salad

5 chicken breasts
4 eggs, hard-boiled, grated
1½ cups sliced grapes
½ cup chopped celery

1 cup mayonnaise
1 cup sour cream
⅔ cup slivered almonds

Boil chicken breasts in enough water to cover in a saucepan until cooked through. Cool and cut into bite-size pieces. Combine chicken, eggs, grapes, and celery in a large bowl; mix well. Stir in a mixture of mayonnaise and sour cream. Chill, covered, until serving time. Stir in almonds just before serving. Serve on croissants or sliced bread. Yields 8–10 servings.

Marsha Harbarger, Riverchase Council (Book 4)

Marinated Chicken Salad

2 large chickens
2 onions, thinly sliced
2 or 3 stalks celery, chopped
Salt to taste
1 green bell pepper, cut into
  strips
1 (8-ounce) jar green salad
  olives, drained
1 (8-ounce) can black olives,
  drained

2 or 3 (16-ounce) cans artichoke
  hearts, cut into thirds
2 (8-ounce) cans sliced
  mushrooms, drained
¼ cup olive oil
1¼ cups vegetable oil
½ cup apple cider vinegar

Rinse chickens well. Combine with onions, celery, salt, and water to cover in large saucepan. Cook until chicken is tender; drain. Cool chicken and chop into bite-size pieces, discarding skin and bones. Combine with green pepper, olives, artichokes, and mushrooms in salad bowl; mix well. Mix olive oil, vegetable oil, and vinegar in small bowl. Add to salad; mix well. Marinate in refrigerator 24 hours, stirring occasionally. Yields 15 servings.

Tom Allen, Birmingham South Cahaba Council (Book 3)

Creole Chicken Salad

1 cup mayonnaise
¾ teaspoon Creole seasoning
¼ teaspoon dill weed
¼ teaspoon paprika
4 cups chopped cooked chicken

1 tablespoon finely chopped bell
  pepper
¼ cup finely chopped celery
¼ cup finely chopped onion
¼ cup sweet pickle relish

Mix mayonnaise, Creole seasoning, dill weed, and paprika in a small bowl. Combine chicken, bell pepper, celery, onion, and pickle relish in a large bowl, tossing to mix. Stir in mayonnaise mixture. Yields 6 servings.

Dot Johnson, Gadsden Life Club (Book 4)

Pot's Macaroni Salad

1 (8-ounce) box macaroni
7 green onions, or 1 small white
  onion, chopped
7 strips celery, chopped
2 hard-boiled eggs, chopped
1 (2.3-ounce) can ripe or green
  olives, chopped
8 slices cheese, chopped

1 (2-ounce) bottle pimentos,
  chopped
2 teaspoons pepper relish
  (or chopped bell pepper)
2 tablespoons mayonnaise
2 tablespoons sour cream
Paprika and celery seeds for
  garnish

Boil macaroni in salted water until tender; drain; rinse in cool water. Place macaroni in medium mixing bowl. Add chopped onions, celery, eggs, olives, cheese, pimentos, and relish to macaroni. Mix well, then add mayonnaise and sour cream. Toss lightly; top with paprika and celery seeds.

C. V. "Pot" Harris, Tuscaloosa Life Member Club (Book 2)

Coca-Cola Salad

3 (3-ounce) packages cream
  cheese, softened
1 cup chopped pecans
1 (29-ounce) can black pitted
  cherries
1 (20-ounce) can crushed
  pineapple

1 (3-ounce) package black cherry
  Jell-O
1 (3-ounce) package strawberry
  Jell-O
2 (6-ounce) bottles Coca-Cola

Cream cheese and nuts; set aside. Drain juices from cherries and pineapple; bring to a boil. Pour over Jell-O and dissolve. Let cool and add Coca-Cola. Cut up cheese and nuts. Combine all ingredients; refrigerate. Serves 24.

Mattie Singleton, Retired, Life Member, Birmingham Central
Council (Book 1)

Ambrosia

1 (14-ounce) can fruit cocktail,
  drained
5 or 6 oranges, peeled, cut up
1 apple, peeled, cut up
1 (8-ounce) can pineapple,
  drained

½ cup sugar
1 cup miniature marshmallows
1 cup chopped pecans
1 cup flaked coconut
½ cup sour cream

Mix all ingredients; chill.

Barbara Davis, Decatur Council (Book 1)

Apple Salad

4 medium apples
2 ribs celery
1 cup seedless purple grapes

1 cup chopped pecans
½–1 cup mayonnaise

Cut apples and celery into small pieces. Cut grapes into halves. Combine apples, celery, grapes, and pecans in a serving bowl and toss to mix. Add mayonnaise; mix well. Serve immediately or chill, covered, until serving time. Yields 8 servings.

Ruth Ann Edson, Gadsden Life Club (Book 4)

Congealed Orange Salad

2 (3-ounce) packages orange
   gelatin
1 cup boiling water
1 pint orange sherbet

1 cup drained Mandarin oranges
1 cup miniature marshmallows
1 cup whipped cream, whipped

Dissolve gelatin in boiling water in bowl. Stir in sherbet until smooth. Chill until partially set. Fold in oranges, marshmallows, and whipped cream. Spoon into dish. Chill until set. Yields 15 servings.

Eulene Miller, Montgomery Council (Book 3)

Congealed Lime Salad

1½ cups chopped pecans
1 dozen marshmallows, chopped, or 1 small bag mini marshmallows
½ cup grated Cracker Barrel cheese

1 (20-ounce) can crushed pineapple, reserve juice
1 (3-ounce) package lime Jell-O
1 cup hot water
1 pint vanilla ice cream, softened

Mix nuts, marshmallows, cheese, and pineapple; add pineapple juice. Dissolve Jell-O in hot water and pour into above mixture; fold in ice cream. Pour into mold; refrigerate.

Rosemary Parker, Birmingham Central Council (Book 2)

Cranberry Salad

1 (12-ounce) bag cranberries, chopped
1½ cups sugar
1 (3-ounce) box strawberry or raspberry Jell-O

1 cup hot water
1 (20-ounce) can crushed pineapple, reserve juice
3–4 oranges, peeled, cut up
½ cup chopped pecans

Combine chopped cranberries and sugar; let set overnight. Next day, mix Jell-O using hot water and juice reserved from pineapple for cold water. Add pineapple, oranges, nuts, and cranberry mixture. Pour into mold and refrigerate.

Rosemary Parker, Birmingham Central Council (Book 2)

Low-Fat Cranberry Salad

2 (3-ounce) packages cherry
  gelatin
1 cup boiling water
2 (16-ounce) cans jellied
  cranberry sauce

1 cup chopped celery
2 apples, peeled, chopped
1 cup chopped pecans

Dissolve gelatin in boiling water in bowl. Heat cranberry sauce in saucepan, beating with rotary beater until smooth. Add to gelatin; mix well. Chill until partially set. Stir in celery, apples, and pecans. Chill until firm. Yields 15 servings.

Jane Green, Riverchase Council (Book 3)

Pink Arctic Frozen Salad

1 (8-ounce) package cream
  cheese, softened
2 tablespoons mayonnaise
2 tablespoons sugar
½ (16-ounce) can whole
  cranberry sauce

1 cup crushed pineapple,
  drained
½ cup chopped English walnuts
1 cup whipped topping

Blend cream cheese, mayonnaise, and sugar in mixer bowl until smooth. Add cranberry sauce, pineapple, and walnuts; mix well. Fold in whipped topping. Spoon into paper-lined muffin cups. Freeze until firm. May remove to plastic bag to store in freezer. Yields 12 servings.

Nancy Morgan, Decatur Council (Book 3)

Tuscan White Bean Salad

2 teaspoons sage
4 teaspoons extra virgin
  olive oil
1 tablespoon dry white wine
1 tablespoon white wine
  vinegar

2 garlic cloves, minced
Black pepper to taste
1 (16-ounce) can cannellini
  beans, rinsed, drained
½ small red onion, chopped

Whisk sage, olive oil, wine, vinegar, garlic, and pepper in a large bowl. Add beans and onion, tossing to coat. Let stand, covered, 2 hours or until the flavors are blended. Yields 4 servings.

Rita Wilson, Birmingham Life Club (Book 4)

3 Bean Salad

1 (1-pound) can cut green
  beans
1 (1-pound) can yellow
  wax beans
1 (1-pound) can red kidney
  beans
1 small onion, chopped
1 small bell pepper, chopped

⅔ cup vinegar
Juice of 1 garlic clove
¾ cup sugar
1 teaspoon salt
½ teaspoon pepper
⅓ cup vegetable oil or Italian
  dressing

Drain all beans and put in large mixing bowl with cover. Mix all other ingredients and pour over beans. Refrigerate overnight. Drain and serve cold. Makes 10–12 servings.

Sherry A. Liles, Future Pioneer, Tri-Cities Council
and Dae Self, Birmingham West Council (Book 1)

Cornbread Salad

1 (10-inch) skillet cornbread
2 small green bell peppers, chopped
2 small purple onions, chopped
1 cup chopped celery
1 (4-ounce) jar chopped pimentos, drained
½ cup sweet pickle relish
1 (16-ounce) can tiny green peas, drained
3 hard-boiled eggs, chopped
4 tomatoes, chopped
8 ounces bacon, crisp-fried, crumbled

Trim bottom from cornbread; crumble remainder into bowl. Add green peppers, onions, celery, pimentos, relish, peas, eggs, tomatoes, and bacon; mix gently.

DRESSING:
1½ cups mayonnaise
¼ cup sweet pickle relish
1 tablespoon sugar
Paprika to taste

Combine mayonnaise, relish, and sugar in small bowl; mix well. Add to salad; toss gently. Sprinkle with paprika. Chill overnight. Yields 16 servings.

Anatalie Watson, Life Member, Decatur Council (Book 3)

Polly's Oriental Salad

1½ cups sliced almonds	1 (15-ounce) package coleslaw
2 (3-ounce) packages oriental-flavor ramen noodles	1½ packages lightly salted sunflower seed kernels
1 bunch green onions, chopped	Oriental Salad Dressing

Arrange almonds on a baking sheet. Toast at 400° for 2–3 minutes or until light brown. Break ramen noodles into small pieces, reserving seasoning packets for Oriental Salad Dressing. Combine almonds, ramen noodles, green onions, coleslaw, and sunflower seed kernels in a large bowl; mix well. Add Oriental Salad Dressing just before serving and toss lightly to mix. Yields 8–10 servings.

ORIENTAL SALAD DRESSING:

2 seasoning packets from ramen noodles	½ cup rice wine vinegar
½ cup canola oil	⅓ cup sugar
	1 teaspoon lemon juice

Combine ramen noodles seasoning, canola oil, wine vinegar, sugar, and lemon juice in a small bowl, and mix well. Yields 1 cup.

Linda McAdams, Shoals Life Club (Book 4)

Romaine and Orange Salad

8 cups torn romaine
1 (11-ounce) can Mandarin
oranges, drained

2 green onions, sliced
¼ cup sliced almonds, toasted
Oil and Vinegar Salad Dressing

Combine romaine, Mandarin oranges, green onions, and almonds in a salad bowl. Pour dressing over top. Toss lightly to mix. Yields 8 servings.

OIL AND VINEGAR SALAD DRESSING:
¼ cup sugar
¼ cup vegetable oil

¼ cup white vinegar

Shake sugar, oil, and vinegar together in a covered jar. Yields ½ cup.

Mrs. Vauline Terry, Tuscaloosa Council (Book 4)

Spicy Coleslaw

2 cups finely shredded red
cabbage
2 cups finely shredded green
cabbage
1 cup finely chopped red onion
¾ cup mayonnaise
1 tablespoon cider vinegar

1 tablespoon fresh lemon juice
1 tablespoon Dijon mustard
¼ teaspoon sugar
¼ teaspoon Worcestershire
⅛ teaspoon white pepper
⅛ teaspoon hot pepper sauce

Mix red cabbage, green cabbage, and red onion in a large bowl. Whisk mayonnaise, cider vinegar, lemon juice, Dijon mustard, sugar, Worcestershire, white pepper, and hot pepper sauce in a small bowl. Pour over cabbage mixture, tossing to coat. Chill, covered, 1 hour or longer. Yields 8 servings.

Jane B. Weatherly, Mobile Council (Book 4)

Cinnamon Pickles

7 pounds cucumbers
1 gallon plus 2 cups water,
  divided
1 cup lime
3 cups light vinegar, divided
1 small bottle red food coloring

¼ cup alum
10 cups sugar
12 cinnamon sticks
1 (8-ounce) package red hot
  cinnamon candies

Peel cucumbers and chop or cut into sticks. Soak in mixture of 1 gallon water and lime in crock for 24 hours; drain and rinse until water runs clear.

Soak cucumbers in ice water to cover in crock for 3 hours; drain.

Combine 1 cup vinegar, food coloring, and alum in large stockpot. Add pickles and water to cover; mix well. Simmer 2 hours; drain.

Combine remaining 2 cups vinegar, remaining 2 cups water, sugar, cinnamon, and cinnamon candies in saucepan. Bring to a boil. Pour over cucumbers in crock; let stand 24 hours.

Drain liquid into saucepan; bring to a boil. Pack cucumbers into sterilized jars. Add hot liquid, leaving ½-inch head space; seal with 2-piece lids. Yields 100 servings.

Hilda Hamilton, Mobile Council (Book 3)

Corn Relish

1 (10-ounce) package frozen
  whole-kernel corn
3 tablespoons white wine
  vinegar
2 tablespoons sugar
½ teaspoon salt

⅛ teaspoon coarsely ground
  black pepper
⅛ teaspoon turmeric
1 (2-ounce) jar diced pimentos,
  drained

Cook corn according to package directions; drain. Stir in next 5 ingredients and cook over medium heat for about 1 minute. Stir in pimentos. Spoon into a bowl; chill for at least 8 hours.

Narice Sutton, Riverchase Council (Book 2)

$200 Salad Dressing

2 teaspoons salt
2 teaspoons celery salt
2 teaspoons paprika
3 teaspoons dry mustard

2 cups oil
½ cup sugar
½ cup vinegar
2 teaspoons grated onion

Put all in double boiler and heat to 98°. Remove from heat and beat while cooling until as thick as soft mustard. Shake well when serving. Do not refrigerate. Makes ¾ quart.

Ann Eberhart, Anniston Council (Book 1)

Kum-Back Salad Dressing

1 teaspoon mustard
2 cloves garlic, minced
¼ onion, grated
Dash of Tabasco
1 lemon, juiced

1 pint mayonnaise
1 tablespoon Worcestershire
1 (10-ounce) bottle chili sauce
Dash of paprika
1 tablespoon black pepper

Mix all ingredients together with electric mixer; chill. Serve over green tossed salad.

Susan Tucker, Huntsville Council (Book 1)

Fruit Salad Dressing

Makes a great topping for fresh fruit salad.

½ cup sugar
4 teaspoons cornstarch
¼ teaspoon salt
1 cup unsweetened pineapple
  juice

¾ cup orange juice
1 tablespoon lemon juice
2 eggs, beaten
2 (3-ounce) packages cream
  cheese, softened

Combine sugar, cornstarch, and salt in saucepan; blend in juices. Cook over low heat, stirring constantly until clear. Remove from heat and slowly stir in eggs; return to low heat and cook 3–5 minutes until slightly thickened. Cool 5 minutes; beat in cream cheese. Can be frozen.

Carol Johnston, Montgomery Council (Book 1)

Vegetables

1919
Candlestick

The first dial telephone exchange is credited to Almon B. Strowger who introduced it in LaPorte, Indiana, in 1892. However, it was many years before switching equipment was sufficiently developed to permit dial installation in larger cities. The advent of the vacuum tube amplifier (or repeater) made lines of any length feasible. With repeaters in the line, transcontinental telephone service opened in 1915. Dial service was coming in strongly, and customers could now dial out themselves, with no need to go through an operator. The first dial phones were candlestick phones. To place a call, you lifted the receiver, waited for dial tone, then dialed. The dial tone was a much lower pitched tone than what we hear today. If the switching equipment was busy, dial tone might take several seconds to come on.

Asparagus au Gratin

2 tablespoons margarine or
  butter
2 tablespoons flour
½ teaspoon salt
Liquid from asparagus plus
  milk to make 1½ cups
1 cup grated Cheddar cheese

4 hard-cooked eggs, sliced
1 pound fresh asparagus, or 1
  box frozen, cooked,
  or 1 (16-ounce) can,
  drained (reserve juice)
½ cup soft bread crumbs
Paprika

Melt butter or margarine in saucepan; blend in flour and salt. Add liquid and cook until thickened, stirring frequently. Remove from heat. Add cheese; stir until cheese is melted. Alternate layers of eggs, asparagus, and cheese sauce. Cover with bread crumbs in greased 2-quart casserole dish. Sprinkle paprika over crumbs. Bake in preheated 350° oven 30 minutes. Serves 4.

Mary Morris, Birmingham Central Council (Book 1)

An exchange is a practical means of communicating between many people who have telephones. The first known exchange linking two major cities was established between New York and Boston in 1883.

English Pea and Asparagus Casserole

1 (15-ounce) can English peas,
   drained
1 (10¾-ounce) can cream of
   mushroom soup
1 (11-ounce) can asparagus
   tips, drained

2 hard-cooked eggs, sliced
Butter
2 cups shredded Cheddar cheese
1 sleeve butter crackers,
   crushed

Layer peas, soup, asparagus, and eggs in a buttered 9x13-inch baking pan. Dot with butter. Top with Cheddar cheese. Sprinkle with cracker crumbs. Bake at 350° for 30 minutes or until bubbly. Yields 8 servings.

Dilla Samuel, Gadsden Life Club (Book 4)

Quick Casserole

1 (15-ounce) can asparagus,
   drained
1 (15-ounce) can English peas,
   drained
1 (15-ounce) can whole potatoes,
   drained

1 (10¾-ounce) can cream of
   celery soup
Buttered bread crumbs
Shredded Cheddar cheese
   (optional)

Combine asparagus, peas, potatoes, and soup in a bowl; mix well. spoon into a baking dish. Top with bread crumbs. Bake at 350° for 30 minutes or until bubbly. You may substitute homemade white sauce for soup or slivered almonds for bread crumbs. May top with shredded Cheddar cheese, if desired. Yields 6 servings.

Faith Kirby Richardson, Gadsden Life Club (Book 4)

Sweet-and-Sour Broccoli

4 medium tomatoes, halved,
seeded
2 pounds broccoli, cut into
¾-inch pieces
1 cup olive oil
2 cups frozen corn, thawed
2 large red bell peppers,
chopped

¼ cup plus 2 tablespoons
lemon juice
¼ cup white wine vinegar
¼ cup sugar
½ teaspoon cinnamon
½ teaspoon pepper
½ cup raisins
½ cup pine nuts

Drain tomatoes on a paper towel. Chill, covered, until ready to serve. Cook broccoli in oil in a skillet over medium heat for 12–15 minutes or until tender. Stir in corn, bell peppers, lemon juice, white wine vinegar, sugar, cinnamon, and pepper. Simmer 5 minutes, stirring occasionally. Stir in raisins and pine nuts. Simmer 2–3 minutes or until thickened, stirring frequently. Spoon mixture into a bowl. Chill, covered, for 2 hours. Spoon broccoli mixture into tomato halves. Yields 8 servings.

Rita Wilson, daughter of Helen Shirley,
Birmingham Life Club (Book 4)

Broccoli and Rice Casserole

2 (10-ounce) packages frozen
chopped broccoli
1 (12-ounce) jar Cheez Whiz
1 (10¾-ounce) can cream of
celery soup

1 (5-ounce) package yellow rice,
cooked
French-fried onions

Steam broccoli in steamer 5 minutes; drain. Combine broccoli, Cheez Whiz, soup, and rice in a bowl and mix gently. Spoon into lightly greased baking dish. Sprinkle with French-fried onions. Bake at 400° for 30 minutes or until brown. Yields 6 servings.

Betty C. Gray, Montgomery Life Club (Book 4)

Swiss Broccoli Casserole

2 (10-ounce) packages frozen
  chopped broccoli
3 hard-boiled eggs, sliced
1 (3-ounce) can French-fried
  onions

1 (10¾-ounce) can cream of
  celery soup
½ soup can milk
½ cup shredded Swiss cheese

Cook broccoli using package directions; drain. Arrange in lightly greased 8x12-inch baking dish. Layer sliced eggs over broccoli; sprinkle with half the onions. Spread with mixture of soup and milk. Sprinkle with shredded cheese. Bake at 350° for 25 minutes. Top with remaining onions. Bake 5 minutes longer. Yields 6 servings.

Note: May substitute Cheddar cheese for Swiss cheese.

Edna Mason, Tuscaloosa Life Club (Book 3)

Broccoli Casserole

2 (10-ounce) packages frozen
  chopped broccoli
2 (10¾-ounce) cans cream of
  mushroom soup
2 eggs
2 cups shredded sharp
  Cheddar cheese, divided

1 onion, chopped
1 tablespoon mayonnaise
1 sleeve butter crackers,
  crushed
1 stick butter, melted

Cook broccoli using package directions; drain. Combine broccoli, soup, eggs, 1 cup Cheddar cheese, onion, and mayonnaise in a bowl; mix gently. Spoon into a lightly greased baking dish. Bake at 350° for 45 minutes or until firm in the middle. Sprinkle remaining 1 cup Cheddar cheese over top. Sprinkle with cracker crumbs. Drizzle with butter. Bake until light brown. Yields 8 servings.

Evelyn Veazey, Opelika Life Club (Book 4)

Stuffed Green Peppers

8–10 green bell peppers
1 cup uncooked regular rice
1 tablespoon shortening
1 pound ground beef
¼ cup chopped onion

¼ cup chopped green bell
  pepper
1½ teaspoons salt
½ teaspoon black pepper

Cut stem ends from peppers and remove seeds. Put peppers into boiling water and cook 2–3 minutes. Remove from water and drain. Cook rice as directed on package. Melt shortening in heavy skillet; add ground beef, onion, chopped pepper, salt, and black pepper. Brown; drain; add to rice and mix. Stuff peppers with mixture. Place in lightly greased baking dish and bake at 350° for 30 minutes. Yields 8–10 servings.

Narice Sutton, Riverchase Council (Book 2)

Squash and Pepper Sauté

2 medium yellow squash,
  sliced
2 medium zucchini, sliced
1 sweet red bell pepper, sliced

¼ cup olive or vegetable oil
1 envelope Italian salad dressing
  mix
3 tablespoons red wine vinegar

Stir-fry squash, zucchini, and bell pepper in olive oil in a skillet over medium-high heat 3–4 minutes or until tender-crisp. Sprinkle with salad dressing mix. Toss to coat. Stir in vinegar. Yields 6 servings.

Hester P. Thompson, Birmingham Life Club (Book 4)

Yellow Squash Casserole

¼ cup butter, melted
1¼ pounds yellow squash,
   thinly sliced
½ teaspoon salt
¼ teaspoon pepper
1 egg, beaten

½ cup mayonnaise
½ cup sour cream
¼ cup chopped onion
1 teaspoon sugar
½ cup shredded sharp cheese

Pour melted butter into a 1½-quart casserole dish; add squash and sprinkle with salt and pepper. Combine egg, mayonnaise, sour cream, onion, and sugar. Mix well and pour over squash. Sprinkle evenly with cheese; bake at 350° for 35–40 minutes. Yields 4–5 servings.

Edwina Hicks, Montgomery Council (Book 1)

Squash Casserole

1 pound yellow squash, sliced
1 small onion, chopped
2 eggs, beaten
1 cup milk
1 cup cracker crumbs

1 cup shredded Cheddar cheese,
   divided
3 tablespoons butter, softened
Salt and pepper to taste

Combine squash and onion with enough water to cover in a saucepan. Cook until tender; drain. Combine squash, onion, eggs, milk, cracker crumbs, ½ cup Cheddar cheese, butter, salt and pepper in a bowl; mix well. Spoon into a buttered baking dish. Sprinkle with remaining ½ cup Cheddar cheese. Bake at 375° for 30 minutes or until firm and brown. Yields 8 servings.

Sheila P. Brothers, Anniston Council (Book 4)

Johnnie's Squash Casserole

2 pounds squash, sliced
3 tablespoons chopped onion
3 eggs, beaten
2 teaspoons parsley flakes

½ teaspoon Tabasco
Salt and pepper to taste
2 cups saltine cracker crumbs
½ cup margarine, melted

Cook squash in water to cover in saucepan 3–5 minutes; drain. Add onion, eggs, parsley flakes, Tabasco, salt and pepper; mix well. Spoon into buttered 1-quart baking dish. Top with mixture of cracker crumbs and margarine. Bake at 350° for 35–40 minutes or until heated through. Yields 6 servings.

Pattie Smith, Gadsden Life Club (Book 3)

Squash Patties

1 cup mashed cooked squash
½ cup self-rising flour
1 egg, beaten
2 tablespoons milk
2 tablespoons chopped onion

1 teaspoon sugar
½ teaspoon salt
Pepper to taste
2 tablespoons oil

Combine squash with flour, egg, milk, onion, sugar, salt and pepper in bowl; mix well. Shape into 16 small patties. Fry on both sides in hot oil in skillet until brown. Yields 4 servings.

Elizabeth Walker, Montgomery Council (Book 3)

Summer Squash Shells

5 slices bacon
6 yellow squash, ends trimmed
3 tomatillos, husked, chopped
¾ cup shredded Monterey
  Jack cheese

½ cup chopped green onions
¾ cup bread crumbs
2–3 tablespoons butter, melted

Fry bacon in a skillet until crisp; drain. Crumble bacon. Combine squash with enough water to cover in a saucepan. Cook just until tender; drain. Let stand until partially cool. Cut squash lengthwise into halves. Scoop pulp into a bowl, reserving squash shells. Add crumbled bacon, tomatillos, Monterey Jack cheese, and green onions to the bowl; mix well. Spoon mixture into squash shells. Arrange in a 9x13-inch baking dish. Sprinkle with bread crumbs. Drizzle with butter. Bake at 350° for 25–30 minutes or until golden brown. You may prepare in advance and chill, covered, until ready to bake. Yields 6 servings.

Rita Wilson, Birmingham Life Club (Book 4)

Squash Dressing

2 cups mashed cooked yellow
  squash
2 cups crumbled cornbread
2 eggs, beaten
1 large onion, chopped

1 (10¾-ounce) can cream of
  chicken soup
½ cup butter, melted
Pepper to taste

Combine squash, cornbread, eggs, onion, soup, butter, and pepper in bowl; mix well. Spoon into buttered baking dish. Bake at 325° for 45 minutes. Yields 6 servings.

Joyce Glenn, Montgomery Council (Book 3)

Eggplant Casserole

1 eggplant, sliced
1½ cups grated sharp cheese,
  divided
1½ cups cracker crumbs,
  divided
1½ cups milk

4 eggs
1 teaspoon salt
½ teaspoon pepper
1 stick margarine, melted,
  divided

Cook eggplant in lightly salted water to cover until mushy; drain. Add all ingredients, reserving ½ cup cheese, ½ cup crumbs, and a small amount of margarine. Mix well. Pour into greased baking dish; sprinkle with reserved cheese, crumbs, and melted butter. Bake at 325°–350° for 30 minutes.

Jane Paulk, Montgomery Council (Book 1)

Cabbage Casserole

4 cups shredded cabbage
1 (28-ounce) can chopped
  tomatoes, undrained
1 teaspoon salt
¼ cup chopped onion
1 tablespoon butter or
  margarine

3 cups cooked regular rice
½ cup cracker crumbs
½ cup shredded Cheddar
  cheese
2 tablespoons butter or
  margarine, melted

Combine first 5 ingredients in a large saucepan; bring to a boil. Reduce heat and simmer 5 minutes. Place ½ of rice in a greased 2-quart casserole dish; top with ½ cabbage mixture. Repeat layers. Combine remaining ingredients, stirring well. Sprinkle over casserole. Bake at 375° for 45 minutes. Yields 8 servings.

Narice Sutton, Riverchase Council (Book 2)

Cabbage Dinner

1 pound ground beef
1 small onion, chopped
1 egg, beaten
1 teaspoon salt
1/4 teaspoon pepper
¼ teaspoon oregano
½ cup bread crumbs
2 tablespoons margarine

4 cups shredded cabbage
1 bell pepper, sliced
4 medium raw potatoes, peeled,
   sliced
Salt and pepper to taste
1 tomato, sliced
½ cup water

Mix first 7 ingredients and form into small meatballs. Brown meatballs on all sides. Drain on paper towels. In 6-quart saucepan, melt margarine over low heat; add cabbage, bell pepper, salt and pepper to taste. Next add potatoes; on top of potatoes, sliced tomato. Add water, then arrange meatballs on top of vegetables. Cover tightly and steam over low heat about 30 minutes, until potatoes are done. Do not stir! Serve directly from saucepan.

Sandy Sprinkle, Anniston Council (Book 1)

Spinach Madeleine

4 (10-ounce) packages frozen
  spinach
¼ cup butter
¼ cup chopped onion
¼ cup all-purpose flour
1 cup evaporated milk
2 (6-ounce) rolls processed cheese
  with jalapeño peppers, cubed

2 teaspoons Worcestershire
½–1 teaspoon pepper
1½ teaspoons celery salt
1½ teaspoons garlic salt
½ cup fine dry bread crumbs
2 teaspoons butter, melted

Cook spinach according to package directions; drain well. Reserve 1 cup liquid; set aside. Melt ¼ cup butter in heavy saucepan over low heat; add onion and sauté until tender. Add flour, stirring until smooth. Cook 1 minute, stirring constantly; gradually add spinach liquid and milk. Cook over medium heat, stirring constantly, until thickened and bubbly.

Add cheese, Worcestershire, and seasonings; stir until cheese melts. Stir spinach into sauce and pour into lightly greased 6x10-inch baking dish. Combine bread crumbs and melted butter; sprinkle over spinach. Bake at 350° for 30 minutes.

Eileen Bevis, Tri-Cities Council (Book 2)

Okra Casserole

1 medium onion, chopped
½ cup (or less) vegetable oil
1 tablespoon flour
Salt and pepper to taste
1 cup water

1¾ cups cut fresh or frozen
  okra
1 (14½-ounce) can tomatoes,
  drained, chopped
1 cup shredded Cheddar cheese

Sauté onion in oil in skillet. Stir in flour, salt and pepper. Add water. Cook until thickened, stirring constantly. Layer okra, white sauce, tomatoes, and cheese in lightly greased baking dish. Bake at 325°–350° for 35 minutes. Yields 4 servings.

Mrs. J. H. McDuffee, Birmingham South Council (Book 3)

Fried Okra

1 pound fresh okra
½ teaspoon salt
¼ teaspoon garlic salt
½ teaspoon pepper

1 tablespoon flour
¾ cup cornmeal
1 egg, slightly beaten
1 cup hot oil

Wash fresh okra and cut into small pieces. Season with salt, garlic salt, and pepper. Mix flour with cornmeal. Dip cut okra into beaten egg, then into cornmeal mixture. Drop into hot oil and fry until tender and brown. Serves 2–4.

Linda Moss, Huntsville Council (Book 2)

Corn Casserole

1 package Mahatma yellow
  rice in a box
1 stick margarine
2 (11-ounce) cans Mexicorn,
  undrained

1 (10¾-ounce) can cream of
  celery soup
1¾ cups grated sharp
  cheese, divided
Paprika for garnish

Prepare rice according to instructions on package. Add margarine; stir until melted.

Stir in corn and soup. Combine 1 cup cheese with mixture; bake 30 minutes at 350°. Remove from oven; sprinkle remaining ¾ cup cheese on top along with a sprinkle of paprika for color.

Jan Cook, Anniston Council (Book 1)

Corn Casserole Olé

4 eggs
2 (16-ounce) cans cream-style
  corn
¾ cup corn oil
½ cup chopped green bell
  pepper

½ cup chopped onion
2 cups shredded Mexican
  Velveeta cheese
1 (7-ounce) package Mexican
  cornbread mix

Beat eggs in mixer bowl. Add corn, corn oil, green pepper, onion, Velveeta cheese, and cornbread mix; mix well. Spoon into 8x12-inch baking dish sprayed with nonstick cooking spray. Bake at 375° for 45 minutes. Cut into squares to serve. Yields 12 servings.

Doris Summersgill, Mobile Life Club (Book 3)

Green Bean Casserole

2 (14½-ounce) cans green
   beans, drained
1 (5-ounce) can sliced water
   chestnuts, drained
1 (4-ounce) can sliced
   mushrooms
1 medium onion, chopped

1 (10¾-ounce) can cream of
   mushroom soup
1 (10¾-ounce) can cream of
   celery soup
Salt to taste
1 cup grated Cheddar cheese

Layer half the beans, water chestnuts, mushrooms, and onion in a
1½- to 2-quart buttered casserole dish. Cover with half the soups,
salt, and cheese. Repeat layers, topping with cheese. Bake at
350°–375° for 30 minutes. Makes 6–8 servings.

Allene Hartzog, Montgomery Council (Book 1)

Lima Beans in Sour Cream

½ cup chopped onion
3 tablespoons butter
1 (2-ounce) jar chopped
   pimento peppers

3 cups lima beans, cooked
½ cup sour cream

Sauté onion in butter; add pimentos and beans and heat through.
Stir in sour cream. Serve immediately.

Diane M. Cook, Montgomery Council (Book 1)

Calico Beans

½ pound ground beef
½ pound bacon, diced
1 large onion, chopped
½ cup ketchup
2 teaspoons salt
2 teaspoons prepared mustard
4 teaspoons cider or white
vinegar
¾ cup firmly packed light
brown sugar

1 (30-ounce) can pork and beans
1 (15-ounce) can garbanzo beans,
drained
1 (10-ounce) package frozen lima
beans, thawed
1 (15-ounce) can kidney beans,
drained
Bacon strips, fried crisp
(optional)

Cook ground beef, bacon, and onion in large skillet until onion is
tender. Drain only if there is a large amount of fat. Stir in ketchup,
salt, mustard, and vinegar. Combine remaining ingredients in a 3-
quart casserole dish. Stir in meat mixture. Cover; bake at 350° for
40 minutes or until bubbly. Garnish with strips of crisp bacon, if
desired.

Mary Ann Davis, Anniston Council (Book 1)

Low-Fat Baked Beans

1 (16-ounce) can pork and
beans
2 tablespoons dark brown
sugar

2 tablespoons ketchup
¼ teaspoon prepared mustard
1 small onion, chopped

Combine ingredients in bowl; mix well. Spoon into baking dish.
Bake at 350° for 25 minutes. Yields 3 servings.

Dottie Richardson, Huntsville Council (Book 3)

Bertha's Baked Beans

1 pound ground beef
1 onion, chopped
1 green bell pepper, chopped
1 cup brown sugar
1 tablespoon prepared mustard
1 cup ketchup

3 (16-ounce) cans pork and
  beans
Dash of Worcestershire
Cooked bacon, crumbled, or
  pineapple slices for top

Combine first 3 ingredients in skillet and brown; drain off all grease. Combine all remaining ingredients along with meat in crockpot. Cook on LOW for 4–6 hours or in regular oven in casserole dish at 350° for 1 hour.

Bertha Johnston, Birmingham Central Council (Book 2)

Make-Ahead Mashed Potatoes

6 medium potatoes, cooked,
  mashed
1 (3-ounce) package cream
  cheese, cubed
½ cup sour cream

¼–½ cup milk
2 tablespoons butter, divided
1 teaspoon onion salt
¼ teaspoon pepper
Paprika (optional)

Combine potatoes, cream cheese, sour cream, milk, 1 tablespoon butter, onion salt, and pepper in a bowl and mash until smooth. Spoon into a greased 9x13-inch or 1½-quart baking dish. Chill, covered, for 8 hours. Melt remaining 1 tablespoon butter. Pour over potatoes. Sprinkle with paprika. Bake at 350° for 45 minutes. Yields 8 servings.

Sue Walton, Birmingham Life Club (Book 4)

Bachelor Potatoes

2 (10-ounce) packages frozen
  hash brown potatoes, thawed
3 cups shredded sharp Cheddar
  cheese, divided

2 cups sour cream
½ cup milk
4 green onions, chopped
Salt and pepper to taste

Combine potatoes, 2¼ cups Cheddar cheese, sour cream, milk, green onions, salt and pepper in a bowl; mix well. Spoon into a baking dish. Sprinkle with remaining ¾ cup Cheddar cheese. Bake at 375° for 45 minutes. Yields 8 servings.

Sue Bryars, Birmingham South Cahaba Council (Book 4)

Irene's Hash Brown Potato Casserole

1 (32-ounce) package frozen
  hash brown potatoes
10 ounces shredded Cheddar
  cheese (2½ cups)
1 (10¾-ounce) can cream of
  chicken soup
1 cup sour cream

½ cup chopped onion
1 stick margarine, melted,
  divided
½ teaspoon each: salt and
  pepper
3 slices bread, crumbled

Combine potatoes, Cheddar cheese, soup, sour cream, onion, ¼ cup margarine, salt and pepper in a bowl, and mix well. Spoon into a greased 9x13-inch baking dish. Mix bread crumbs with remaining ¼ cup margarine in a bowl. Sprinkle over top of prepared dish. Bake at 350° for 70 minutes. Yields 12 servings.

Virginia Bowen, Shoals Life Club (Book 4)

Potato Casserole

1 medium onion, chopped
3 tablespoons butter
1 (10¾-ounce) can cream of
  chicken soup
¾ can water

1 (3-ounce) package cream
  cheese, cubed
1 (26-ounce) package frozen
  shoestring fries, divided
¾ cup grated cheese, divided

Sauté onion in butter; add soup and water; mix until smooth. Chip
in cream cheese, and stir; cook about 5 minutes or till cheese has
melted. Lightly butter a 9x9-inch casserole; add layer of potatoes,
then sauce; lightly sprinkle with grated cheese. Layer again potatoes, sauce, and cheese. Bake at 350° for 45 minutes.

Hazel Campbell, Birmingham South Council (Book 1)

Creamy Irish Potato Casserole

6–8 Irish potatoes
½ cup butter, melted
2 (10¾-ounce) cans cream of
  mushroom soup

Salt and coarsely ground pepper
  to taste
1 cup shredded Cheddar cheese

Peel potatoes and slice ¼ inch thick. Combine with butter, soup,
salt and pepper in bowl; mix well. Spoon into lightly greased baking dish. Bake at 350° until potatoes are tender. Top with cheese.
Bake several minutes longer. Yields 10 servings.

Note: May substitute cream of chicken soup for cream of mushroom
soup.

Beckie Fomby, Montgomery Council (Book 3)

Glazed Sweet Potatoes

5 or 6 medium sweet potatoes ½ teaspoon salt
2 tablespoons water 2 tablespoons butter or
1 cup sugar margarine

Wash sweet potatoes and boil until nearly done. Drain; remove skins. Cut lengthwise into slices and arrange in baking dish. Make a syrup of boiling water, sugar, and salt. Add butter or margarine. Pour syrup over sweet potatoes. Bake at 350° for about 35 minutes or until potatoes are glazed. Baste with syrup 2 or 3 times during baking. Yields 4 servings.

Narice Sutton, Riverchase Council (Book 2)

Crunchy Sweet Potato Casserole

3 cups mashed cooked sweet ½ cup evaporated milk
  potatoes ½ cup butter, melted
1 cup sugar 1 teaspoon vanilla extract
2 eggs

Combine sweet potatoes, sugar, eggs, evaporated milk, butter, and vanilla in bowl; mix well. Spoon into buttered baking dish.

TOPPING:
1 cup packed brown sugar ⅓ cup butter, melted
⅓ cup flour ½–1 cup chopped pecans

Combine brown sugar, flour, butter, and pecans in bowl. Spread over sweet potatoes. Bake at 350° for 30 minutes. Yields 8 servings.

Note: May substitute milk for evaporated milk.

Hazel Campbell, Birmingham Life Club (Book 3)

Sweet Potato and Coconut Casserole

4 cups mashed cooked sweet potatoes
1 cup sugar
½ cup milk
¾ cup margarine, softened, divided

1 cup flaked coconut
1 teaspoon vanilla extract
1 cup chopped pecans
½ cup flour
1 cup packed brown sugar

Combine sweet potatoes, sugar, milk, ½ cup margarine, coconut, and vanilla in bowl; mix well. Spoon into buttered baking dish. Mix pecans, remaining ¼ cup margarine, flour, and brown sugar in small bowl. Sprinkle over casserole. Bake at 400° for 15 minutes. Yields 8 servings.

Ethel Beasley, Birmingham Life Club (Book 3)

Sweet Potato Soufflé

3 cups mashed cooked sweet potatoes
1 cup sugar
½ cup milk
1 stick butter, melted, divided
2 eggs, beaten

1 teaspoon orange extract
1 teaspoon pineapple extract
1 cup packed brown sugar
½ cup all-purpose flour
1 cup chopped pecans

Combine sweet potatoes, sugar, milk, ¼ cup butter, eggs, and extracts in a bowl; mix well. Mix brown sugar and flour in a bowl. Sprinkle over prepared dish. Drizzle with remaining butter. Sprinkle with pecans. Bake at 350° for 30–35 minutes or until bubbly. Yields 8 servings.

Carolyn Wheeler, Selma Life Club (Book 4)

Piccadilly Carrot Soufflé

3 pounds baby carrots,
  steamed, drained
2 cups sugar
¼ cup all-purpose flour
1 tablespoon baking powder

1 tablespoon vanilla extract
6 eggs
2 sticks margarine, melted
Confectioners' sugar

Process carrots in food processor container until finely chopped. Add sugar, flour, baking powder, and vanilla and process until smooth. Add eggs and margarine and process until blended. Spoon into a buttered 9x13-inch baking pan. Bake at 350° for 1¼ hours. Dust top with confectioners' sugar. Yields 12 servings.

Virginia Greene, Birmingham South Life Club (Book 4)

Vegetable Casserole

2 (15-ounce) cans Veg-All,
  drained
1 cup chopped onion
1 cup chopped water chestnuts

1 cup grated Cheddar cheese
¾ cup mayonnaise
1 roll Ritz Crackers, crushed
1 stick margarine, melted

Mix vegetables, onion, water chestnuts, Cheddar cheese, and mayonnaise. Pour into lightly greased casserole dish. Mix crackers with melted margarine. Top casserole with cracker mixture; bake at 350° for 30 minutes.

Mary C. Martin, Birmingham East Council (Book 1)

Easy Vidalia Onion Casserole

2 Vidalia onions, thinly sliced
1 (10¾-ounce) can cream of
mushroom soup

1 cup crushed potato chips
½ cup shredded Cheddar
cheese

Layer onions, soup, chips, and cheese in baking dish. Bake at 350° for 45 minutes. Yields 4 servings.

Shirley Waldrop, Birmingham Life Club (Book 3)

Vidalia Onion Casserole

1 (10¾-ounce) can cream of
chicken soup
1 cup sour cream
2 medium Vidalia onions,
sliced

Grated Parmesan cheese
1 sleeve butter crackers,
crushed
¼ stick butter or margarine,
melted

Combine soup and sour cream in a bowl; mix well. Add onions and toss to coat. Spoon into a baking dish. Sprinkle with Parmesan cheese. Combine cracker crumbs and butter in a bowl; mix well. Sprinkle over top of prepared dish. Bake at 300°–325° for 35 minutes. Yields 4–6 servings.

Mary Ruth Thompson, Shoals Life Club (Book 4)

Fresh Tomato Pie

2 cups baking mix
¾ cup milk
1 teaspoon basil
1 teaspoon chives
1 teaspoon parsley
4 medium tomatoes, sliced

1 green bell pepper, sliced
   (optional)
1½ cups shredded sharp
   Cheddar cheese
½ cup mayonnaise

Combine baking mix and milk in a bowl and stir until blended. Press over bottom and side of a greased 9-inch pie plate. (You may use a frozen 9-inch pie shell.) Combine basil, chives, and parsley in a small bowl; mix well. Alternate layers of tomato and bell pepper, sprinkling herb mixture over each layer. Combine Cheddar cheese and mayonnaise in a bowl; mix well. Spread over top of prepared dish. Bake at 400° for 20–25 minutes or until crust and top are golden brown. Let stand 10 minutes before serving. Yields 4 servings.

Frankie Vaughn, Selma Life Club (Book 4)

Fried Green Tomatoes

4 large firm green tomatoes
½ cup all-purpose flour or
   cornmeal

1 teaspoon salt
¼ teaspoon pepper
Bacon drippings or shortening

Cut tomatoes in ¼-inch slices. Mix flour or cornmeal with salt and pepper. Coat tomatoes with this mixture. Place in heavy skillet, containing hot bacon drippings or shortening. Fry slowly until brown, turning once. Yields 6 servings.

Narice Sutton, Riverchase Council (Book 2)

Cheese Frosted Cauliflower

1 head cauliflower
½ cup mayonnaise

2 teaspoons prepared mustard
¾ cup shredded sharp cheese

Cook cauliflower in boiling water, leaving whole; drain well. Place in a shallow pan and frost with mayonnaise mixed with mustard. Sprinkle on cheese; bake at 350° until cheese melts, about 10 minutes.

Nancy S. Black, Decatur Council (Book 1)

Hot Pineapple Casserole

2 (20-ounce) cans pineapple
    tidbits, undrained
5 tablespoons flour
1 cup sugar

24 butter crackers, crushed
½ cup margarine, melted
1 cup shredded sharp Cheddar
    cheese, divided

Spread pineapple in lightly greased 9x13-inch baking dish. Sprinkle with flour and sugar. Sprinkle mixture of cracker crumbs, melted margarine, and half the cheese over pineapple; top with remaining cheese. Bake at 350° for 30 minutes. Yields 12 servings.

Barbara Rosser, Montgomery Council (Book 3)

Baked Apples

10–12 medium Gala apples   **Margarine or butter**
Sugar to taste

Peel, core, and cut apples into quarters. Arrange over bottom of a buttered 9x13-inch glass baking dish. Sprinkle generously with sugar. Dot generously with margarine. Bake at 450° for 45–60 minutes, stirring after 25 minutes. Yields 8–10 servings.

Jack D. Phillips, Birmingham South Life Club (Book 4)

Apple Cheese Casserole

1 stick margarine, softened   **¾ cup all-purpose flour**
½–1 cup sugar   **1 (20-ounce) can sliced apples**
8 ounces Velveeta or sharp
  Cheddar cheese, shredded

Cream margarine and sugar in a mixing bowl until light and fluffy. Add cheese and flour; mix well. Pour apples evenly in a buttered baking dish. Spread cheese mixture over top. Bake at 350° for 30 minutes. Yields 4–6 servings.

Gussie Evans, Mobile Council (Book 4)

Pasta, Rice, Etc.

1930
Single Handset
Oval-Base

Although the single handset containing both the receiver and transmitter was developed for operators and repairmen by 1878, it wasn't until 1927 that the single handset telephone was introduced to the general public. The 1927 model had a round base. In 1930 it was redesigned with an elongated base made to compliment the long handset. The dial was also recessed into the front of the phone. Like the Candlestick, only the switchhook and switch were contained in the phone. The network and ringer were contained in a subset that was mounted on the wall. The subsets contained a new induction coil that would be used for nearly twenty years.

Vegetable Lasagna

1 medium zucchini, coarsely
  chopped
8 ounces fresh mushrooms,
  sliced
1 onion, coarsely chopped
1 large green bell pepper,
  coarsely chopped
1 (14½-ounce) can Italian
  tomatoes
Italian seasoning to taste

2 garlic cloves, pressed
1 (10-ounce) package frozen
  chopped spinach, thawed
7 or 8 lasagna noodles, cooked
1 (28-ounce) jar spaghetti sauce
4 cups shredded mozzarella
  cheese
1 (16-ounce) container cottage
  cheese

Combine zucchini, mushrooms, onion, bell pepper, tomatoes, Italian seasoning, and garlic in a large skillet. Cook until vegetables are tender and liquid has almost completely evaporated. Drain spinach, pressing out excess moisture. Layer ½ of noodles, ½ of spaghetti sauce, vegetable mixture, ½ of mozzarella cheese, remaining noodles, remaining spaghetti sauce, spinach, cottage cheese, and remaining mozzarella cheese in a 9x13-inch baking dish sprayed with nonstick cooking spray. Bake at 375° for 30 minutes. Yields 10–12 servings.

Kelli Lee, Anniston Council (Book 4)

Lasagna

1½–2 pounds ground beef
1 clove garlic, or 1 teaspoon
  garlic salt
1 tablespoon sweet basil
1½ teaspoons salt (omit if
  using garlic salt)
1 cup sugar
1 (15-ounce) can tomato sauce
1 (12-ounce) can tomato paste
1 (10- or 16-ounce) box lasagna
  noodles

2 eggs
3 cups cottage cheese
½ cup grated Romano cheese
1¼ tablespoons parsley flakes
1 teaspoon salt
½ teaspoon pepper
1 pound shredded mozzarella
  cheese

Brown meat; pour off grease. Add next 6 ingredients. Simmer, uncovered, 30 minutes. Cook noodles until al dente in a large amount of boiling salted water. Drain and rinse. In a bowl, beat eggs; add cottage cheese, Romano cheese, parsley flakes, salt, and pepper. Now, you are ready to layer lasagna.

Put some sauce on bottom of a 9x13-inch pan, then ½ the noodles, ½ the remaining sauce, ½ the cottage cheese mixture; repeat, ending with sauce on top layer. Top with mozzarella cheese. Bake at 375° for 30 minutes. Serves 8–10.

Rosemary Parker, Birmingham Central Council (Book 2)

Baked Pasta

1 (16-ounce) package shell pasta
1 (10¾-ounce) can cream of
  celery soup
1¼ cups milk
1 envelope Italian salad
  dressing mix
1 (15-ounce) container ricotta
  cheese
¾ cup grated Parmesan cheese,
  divided
2 (16-ounce) packages frozen
  mixed vegetables, thawed

Cook pasta using package directions; drain. Combine soup, milk, and dressing mix in a large bowl; mix well. Add ricotta cheese and ½ cup Parmesan cheese; mix well. Add cooked pasta and vegetables; mix well. Spoon into a 9x13-inch baking dish sprayed with nonstick cooking spray. Sprinkle remaining ¼ cup Parmesan cheese over top. Bake at 350° for 45–50 minutes or until heated through. Yields 6–8 servings.

Eula Mae Watson, Gadsden Life Club (Book 4)

Baked Ziti

3 cups spaghetti sauce
1 (16-ounce) container ricotta
  cheese
3 cups shredded mozzarella
  cheese, divided
½ cup ziti, cooked
½ cup grated Parmesan

Spread ½ the spaghetti sauce over bottom of 9x13-inch baking dish. Combine ricotta cheese and 1½ cups mozzarella cheese in a bowl; mix well. Add ziti; mix well. Spoon over spaghetti sauce. Spread remaining spaghetti sauce over cheese mixture. Sprinkle remaining 1½ cups mozzarella cheese and Parmesan cheese over top. Bake at 350° for 15–20 minutes, or until heated through. Let stand 10 minutes.

Judy Evans, Decatur Council (Book 4)

Cannelloni

½ pound ground beef
¼ pound bulk sausage
¼ cup chopped onion
½ cup grated Parmesan
 cheese, divided
3 eggs, beaten
¼ cup chopped parsley
¼ teaspoon crushed oregano
 leaves

½ teaspoon garlic salt
8 manicotti shells, uncooked
2 (14½-ounce) cans tomatoes
1 (8-ounce) can tomato sauce
¼ cup water
1 (4-ounce) package shredded
 mozzarella cheese

Brown meat; drain. Add onion; cook until tender. Stir in ¼ cup Parmesan cheese, eggs, parsley, and seasonings. Fill manicotti shells; place in lightly greased 6x10-inch baking dish. Pour in combined tomatoes, tomato sauce, and water over manicotti; sprinkle with remaining Parmesan cheese. Cover with aluminum foil; bake at 350° for 1 hour. Top with mozzarella cheese. Continue baking until cheese is melted. Serves 4.

Becky Cook, Huntsville Council (Book 1)

Noodles with Shrimp Scampi Sauce

3¾ cups wide egg noodles	1 tablespoon fresh lemon juice
⅔ cup butter or margarine	Salt and freshly ground pepper
2 garlic cloves, minced	to taste
1 teaspoon basil	2 teaspoons freshly chopped
¾ pound fresh shrimp,	parsley
peeled, deveined	Lemon wedges

Cook noodles using package directions; drain and set aside. Melt butter in a large skillet. Add garlic and basil and sauté over low heat. Add shrimp and cook 3–4 minutes or until shrimp turn pink, stirring constantly. Add lemon juice, salt, pepper, and parsley. Add noodles and toss to mix well. Serve immediately with lemon wedges. Yields 4 servings.

Anatalie Watson Fogg, Decatur Council (Book 4)

 The very first American 911 call was placed on February 16, 1968, in Haleyville, Alabama. Alabama Speaker of the House, Rankin Fite, made the first call from another city hall room. It was answered by Congressman Tom Bevill on a bright red telephone located in the police department. Bob Gallagher, president of the Alabama Telephone Company initiated and directed the overall 911 effort. Bob Fitzgerald, plant manager, designed and engineered the needed circuitry for the first U.S. 911 system.

Shrimp and Pasta Packages

16 ounces angel hair pasta,
  cooked, drained
48 cooked, peeled shrimp
2 sticks butter
1 red bell pepper, chopped
8 ounces mushrooms, sliced
½ cup chopped green onions
½ cup chopped fresh parsley

3 tablespoons soy sauce
2 teaspoons Worcestershire
2 teaspoons garlic salt
½ teaspoon ginger
Dash of Tabasco
1 (14-ounce) can chicken broth
15 fresh snow peas, sliced

Cut aluminum foil to 8 (12x12-inch) squares. Divide pasta evenly into 8 portions and place in center of each foil square. Place 6 shrimp on top of each portion of pasta.

Melt butter in a large skillet. Add bell pepper, mushrooms, green onions, and parsley. Sauté until tender. Add soy sauce, Worcestershire, garlic salt, ginger, and Tabasco, and mix well. Cook 2 minutes. Add chicken broth; cook 3 minutes. Spoon mixture evenly over each portion of pasta and shrimp. Top with snow peas. Bring sides of foil squares up and fold over. Seal the two open ends. Place foil packages on a baking sheet. Bake at 350° for 20 minutes. Remove from oven, cut an X in the top of each foil package and pull edges away. Yields 8 servings.

Rita Wilson, Birmingham Life Club (Book 4)

Inside-Out Ravioli

1 pound ground beef
½ cup chopped onion
1 clove garlic, minced
2 (10-ounce) packages frozen
  spinach
1 (8-ounce) jar Prego sauce
1 (8-ounce) can tomato sauce
1 (6-ounce) can tomato paste
½ teaspoon salt
Dash of pepper

1 (8-ounce) package shell
  macaroni
1 cup shredded sharp Cheddar
  cheese
½ cup shredded American
  cheese
½ cup bread crumbs
2 eggs, well beaten
1 (12-ounce) package shredded
  mozzarella cheese, divided

Brown ground beef, onion, and garlic; drain. Cook spinach according to package directions; drain, saving 1 cup liquid. Add liquid to meat. Mix Prego, tomato sauce, tomato paste, salt, and pepper together; add cooked spinach. Add to meat. Simmer 45 minutes.

Cook and drain shell macaroni. Add cheese, bread crumbs, eggs, and some mozzarella. Mix with meat mixture, reserving about 1 cup meat mixture; put in a large casserole dish. Top with meat mixture. Bake at 350° for 30 minutes. After about 20 minutes, top with remaining mozzarella and bake 10 minutes longer.

Betsy Burrell, Birmingham East Council (Book 2)

Pepperoni Spaghetti

1 medium onion, chopped
½ cup chopped green bell
  pepper
½ cup reduced-fat margarine
1 (16-ounce) package spaghetti,
  cooked
1 (32-ounce) jar chunky
  garden-style spaghetti sauce

1 pound ground beef
1 (12-ounce) package shredded
  mozzarella cheese
1 (8-ounce) package sliced
  pepperoni

Sauté onion and green pepper in margarine in small skillet until tender. Combine with spaghetti in bowl; mix gently. Spread in baking dish sprayed with nonstick cooking spray. Spread with spaghetti sauce. Brown ground beef in skillet, stirring until crumbly; drain. Sprinkle over spaghetti sauce. Top with cheese and pepperoni. Bake at 350° for 30 minutes. Yields 6 servings.

Mary Howle, Anniston Council (Book 3)

Macaroni and Cheese

2½ cups water
1½ teaspoons salt, divided
1 cup uncooked macaroni
¼ pound shredded sharp
  Cheddar cheese

¼ pound shredded mild
  Cheddar cheese
4 tablespoons butter, melted
2 eggs, beaten
2 cups milk

Bring water and 1 teaspoon salt to a boil; add macaroni and cook until tender, about 8 minutes. Drain and let cool. Put a layer of macaroni in a baking dish and cover with a layer of mixed cheeses. Repeat. Drizzle melted butter over macaroni. Combine eggs, milk, and remaining ½ teaspoon salt. Pour over macaroni and bake at 350° for 30 minutes.

Brenda Etheredge, Mobile Council (Book 1)

Spicy Jambalaya

1 package Zatarain's Jambalaya
  Mix
1 pound smoked sausage,
  chopped
1 pound small shrimp,
  deveined
1 chicken breast, cooked,
  chopped

1 small onion, chopped
1 tablespoon chopped green bell
  pepper
1 tablespoon chopped pimento
1 clove garlic, minced
Salt and black pepper to taste
Crushed red pepper flakes and
  cayenne pepper to taste

Prepare jambalaya mix using package directions. Sauté sausage in skillet. Add to jambalaya with shrimp, chicken, onion, green pepper, pimento, garlic, salt and black pepper; mix well. Sprinkle with crushed red pepper. Simmer, covered, for 45–60 minutes or until rice is tender. Season with cayenne pepper. Yields 8 servings.

Note: May substitute turkey for chicken.

Helen Smith, Birmingham Metro Council (Book 3)

Bacon Fried Rice

1 bag (boil-in-bag) rice
6 slices bacon, cut in eighths
1 cup sliced fresh mushrooms
½ cup sliced green onions

1 egg, slightly beaten
½ cup sliced water chestnuts
3 tablespoons soy sauce

Cook rice according to package directions; drain. While rice is cooking, sauté bacon in wok or 10-inch skillet until almost crisp. Remove bacon pieces and let drain on paper towels. Pour off all but ¼ cup drippings. Stir mushrooms and onions into hot fat. Stir-fry 2–3 minutes or until mushrooms are limp. Add rice; continue to stir-fry until rice is hot, 3–5 minutes. Push rice to one side of skillet. Pour egg into other side and scramble. Add water chestnuts, soy sauce, and reserved bacon pieces to skillet; mix well. Makes 4 (⅔-cup) servings.

Jane Horton, Birmingham Central Council (Book 1)

Red Beans and Rice

½ cup chopped onion
½ cup chopped green bell
  pepper
1 clove garlic
2 tablespoons margarine

1 (16-ounce) can red kidney
  beans
2 cups cooked rice
1 teaspoon salt
⅛ teaspoon pepper

Sauté onion, pepper, and garlic in margarine until tender. Remove garlic. Add remaining ingredients; simmer together 5 minutes to blend flavors. Serves 4–6.

Flo Thompson, Montgomery Council (Book 1)

Easy Red Beans and Rice

1 pound dried red kidney
  beans
1 large onion, chopped
1 teaspoon garlic salt, or to
  taste
1½ tablespoons chili powder

1 tablespoon parsley
Salt to taste
1 pound smoked sausage, cut
  into bite-size pieces
Hot cooked rice

Rinse and sort beans. Combine beans, onion, garlic salt, chili powder, parsley, and salt in a large saucepan. Cook using package directions on beans until the beans are almost tender. Stir in sausage. Cook until beans are tender. Remove ½ cup of beans and place in a bowl; mash. Stir into bean mixture. Simmer until mixture thickens. Serve over hot cooked rice. Yields 4–6 servings.

Rubie McInnis, Birmingham Life Club (Book 4)

Mushroom Rice Casserole

1½ sticks butter
2 cups rice
2 (10¾-ounce) cans French
  onion soup
2 (14-ounce) cans beef
  consommé

2 (3-ounce) jars sliced
  mushrooms, drained
Pepper to taste

Heat butter in a 9x13-inch baking dish in the oven until melted. Add rice, soup, consommé, mushrooms, and pepper; mix well. Bake, covered, at 350° for 45–60 minutes or until bubbly. Yields 10–12 servings.

Mrs. Edward K. Horton, Sr., Mobile Council (Book 4)

Murphies Crabmeat Quiche

3 eggs, slightly beaten
1 cup sour cream
½ teaspoon Worcestershire
¾ teaspoon salt
1 cup coarsely shredded Swiss
  cheese

1 (6½-ounce) can crabmeat,
  drained, finely flaked
1 (3½-ounce) can French-fried
  onions
1 (9-inch) pie shell, baked

To the slightly beaten eggs, add sour cream, Worcestershire, and salt; mix well. Then add shredded cheese, crabmeat, and onions. Pour into baked pie shell. Bake 55–60 minutes at 300° or until custard is set and a knife inserted in center comes out clean. Serve hot.

Anne Spragins, Birmingham East Council (Book 1)

Sue's Mexican Quiche

1 (9- to 10-inch) pie shell,
  unbaked
8 ounces ground sausage
½ cup chopped green onions
½ cup chopped jalapeño
  peppers

1 (8-ounce) package shredded
  Cheddar cheese
1 cup evaporated milk
2 tablespoons self-rising flour
4 eggs, beaten

Bake pie shell at 325° for 5–10 minutes or until partially cooked.
Brown sausage with green onions in skillet, stirring until sausage
is crumbly; drain. Add jalapeño peppers; set aside. Combine
cheese, evaporated milk, and flour in saucepan. Cook until cheese
melts, stirring to blend well. Stir a small amount of hot mixture
into eggs; stir eggs into hot mixture. Stir in sausage mixture.
Spoon into pie shell. Bake 20–25 minutes or until set. Let stand 10
minutes before serving. Yields 6 servings.

Mera Roberts, Mobile Life Club (Book 3)

Meats

1937
"300" Series

An innovation in telephone design was the placing of the bell in the base of the "300" Series desk set. The "300" Series was the first model that included the ringer, coil, and capacitor in the base, forming a complete phone in one package. Previous models required an external subset that contained these components. The "300" Series was made from 1936 until 1954. Earlier versions had housings made of die-cast metal but thermo-plastic was substituted in the early 1940s due to the onset of World War II.

Soon crossbar switching was introduced, and automation came to long-distance switching. Dialed routing codes soon gave way to the familiar area codes, which the switch itself could translate into the needed routing information. Call completion time dropped to 10–20 seconds.

Quick and Easy Meatloaf

1½ pounds ground beef   1 envelope dry onion soup mix
1 or 2 large crackers, crumbled   1 egg
½ cup ketchup or BBQ sauce

Mix all ingredients and bake in 350° oven for approximately 30 minutes or until done. If desired, pour small amount of ketchup or BBQ sauce on top of meatloaf before cooking.

Mary C. Martin, Birmingham East Council (Book 1)

Stuffed Meatloaf

8 ounces fresh mushrooms, sliced   ½ teaspoon dried thyme
1 medium onion, chopped   2 teaspoons salt, divided
2 tablespoons butter or margarine   ¼ teaspoon pepper, divided
2 cups soft bread crumbs   2 eggs
2 tablespoons chopped fresh parsley   2 tablespoons milk
    ¼ cup ketchup
    1 teaspoon brown sugar
    1½ pounds lean ground beef

Sauté mushrooms and onion in butter in a skillet 3 minutes or until tender. Add bread crumbs, parsley, thyme, ½ teaspoon salt, and ⅛ teaspoon pepper; mix well. Sauté until bread crumbs are light brown. Beat eggs, milk, ketchup, remaining 1½ teaspoons salt, ⅛ teaspoon pepper, and brown sugar together in a large bowl. Add ground beef and mix well. Press ½ of the ground beef mixture over bottom of a greased 5x9-inch loaf pan. Spoon bread crumb mixture over ground beef layer. Press remaining ground beef mixture over bread crumb mixture gently. Bake at 350° for 1 hour or until cooked through; drain. Yields 6 servings.

Hester P. Thompson, Birmingham Life Club (Book 4)

Cottage Meatloaf

¾ cup ketchup, divided
⅓ cup tomato juice
½ teaspoon salt
½ teaspoon black pepper
⅛ teaspoon red pepper
2 eggs, beaten

¾ cup fresh bread crumbs
¼ cup finely chopped onion
2½ teaspoons mustard, divided
1½ pounds lean ground beef
2 teaspoons brown sugar

Line a 5x9-inch loaf pan with foil. Combine ½ cup ketchup, tomato juice, salt, black pepper, red pepper, eggs, bread crumbs, onion, and 2 teaspoons mustard in a bowl; mix well. Add ground beef and mix well. Pack into prepared pan. Combine remaining ¼ cup ketchup, ½ teaspoon mustard, and brown sugar in a small bowl; mix well. Spread over top of meatloaf. Bake at 400° for 35–45 minutes or until cooked through. Skim off fat. Let stand 5 minutes. Yields 5–6 servings.

Mary Alice Neal, Birmingham Life Club (Book 4)

Oatmeal Meatloaf

1 pound ground beef
1¼ cups oatmeal
2¼ teaspoons salt
¼ teaspoon celery salt
¼ teaspoon pepper
1 egg, well beaten

1 teaspoon poultry seasoning
1 cup evaporated milk
⅔ cup canned tomatoes, or 1
   (8-ounce) can tomato sauce
¼ cup minced onion

Combine all ingredients; pack into a greased loaf pan. Bake at 350° for 1 hour.

Jamima Edney, Birmingham South Council (Book 2)

Firecracker Casserole

2 pounds ground beef
1 large onion, chopped
2 tablespoons chili powder
2 teaspoons ground cumin
1 teaspoon salt
1 (15-ounce) can chili beans

6 tortillas
1½ cups shredded Cheddar
  cheese
1 (10-ounce) can Ro-Tel
  tomatoes

Cook ground beef and onion until done; drain drippings. Add chili powder, cumin, and salt. Stir well. Cook over low heat 10 minutes. Spoon meat mixture into 9x13-inch casserole dish. Layer beans, tortillas, and cheese over meat mixture. Pour Ro-Tel tomatoes on top. Cover baking pan and refrigerate overnight; bake uncovered at 350° for 1 hour. Yields 8–10 servings.

Gloria H. Ramage, Birmingham South Council (Book 1)

Ground Chuck Bake

1½ pounds ground chuck
¼ cup rolled oats
Salt and pepper to taste
½ cup flour
2 tablespoons oil

2 (10-ounce) cans cream of
  mushroom soup
1 soup can water
1 envelope onion soup mix

Combine ground chuck, oats, salt and pepper in bowl; mix well. Press into 10x15-inch pan. Chill, covered, overnight.

Cut into squares. Coat with flour. Brown on both sides in oil in skillet; remove to baking dish. Combine soup, water, and soup mix in bowl; mix well. Spread over squares. Bake at 300° for 20–30 minutes or until done to taste. Yields 6 servings.

Hazel Campbell, Birmingham Life Club (Book 3)

Meat and Potato Casserole

6 slices bacon
1 pound ground beef
⅓ cup chopped onion
1 cup dry bread cubes
¼ cup ketchup
1 teaspoon chili powder
½ teaspoon pepper

4 cups hot mashed cooked
  potatoes
½ cup shredded Cheddar
  cheese
1 egg, beaten
1 teaspoon salt

Fry bacon in skillet until crisp; remove to paper towel to drain. Add ground beef and onion to drippings in skillet. Cook until ground beef is brown and crumbly. Add bread cubes, ketchup, chili powder, and pepper; mix well. Mash potatoes with cheese, egg, and salt in bowl. Spread half the potato mixture in greased 1½-quart baking dish. Add ground beef mixture; top with remaining potato mixture. Bake at 350° for 30 minutes. Crumble bacon over top. Yields 6 servings.

Margaret McHale, Birmingham Life Club (Book 3)

Farmhouse Muffins

1 (8-count) package refrigerated
  buttermilk biscuits
1 pound ground beef or chuck
½ cup ketchup

3 tablespoons brown sugar
½ teaspoon chili powder
1 cup shredded sharp Cheddar
  cheese

Separate biscuits and flatten into circles. Press each biscuit over bottom and up side of a greased muffin cup. Brown ground beef in a skillet, stirring until crumbly; drain. Combine ketchup, brown sugar, and chili powder in a bowl; mix well. Stir in cooked ground beef. Spoon ¼ cup ground beef mixture into each biscuit-lined muffin cup. Sprinkle with cheese. Bake at 375° for 18–20 minutes. Yields 8 servings.

Debbie Morris, Birmingham South Cahaba Council (Book 4)

Three-Meat Baked Beans

8 ounces Polish sausage
8 ounces ground beef
3 tablespoons chopped onion
5 slices bacon, crisp-fried,
  crumbled
2 (16-ounce) cans pork and
  beans

⅓ cup ketchup
¼ cup packed brown sugar
2 tablespoons molasses
1½ teaspoons Worcestershire
1½ teaspoons prepared
  mustard

Cut sausage into ¼-inch slices. Brown in skillet. Remove sausage with slotted spoon and drain skillet. Add ground beef and onion to skillet. Cook until ground beef is brown and crumbly, stirring frequently; drain. Add sausage, bacon, pork and beans, ketchup, brown sugar, molasses, Worcestershire, and mustard; mix well. Spoon into lightly greased 2-quart baking dish. Bake at 350° for 30 minutes. Yields 8 servings.

Jane Green, Riverchase Council (Book 3)

Ground Beef Casserole

1 pound ground chuck
1 garlic clove, minced
Salt and pepper to taste
1 teaspoon sugar
1 (15-ounce) can tomato sauce
1 cup sour cream

6 ounces cream cheese, softened
1 bunch green onions, chopped
2 cups shredded Cheddar cheese,
   divided
1 (5-ounce) package egg noodles

Brown ground chuck in a skillet, stirring until crumbly. Stir in garlic, salt, pepper, sugar, and tomato sauce. Simmer 15 minutes. Combine sour cream, cream cheese, green onions, and 1½ cups Cheddar cheese and mix well. Cook noodles using package directions; drain. Alternate layers of noodles, ground chuck mixture, and cheese mixture in a baking dish until all ingredients are used, ending with cheese mixture. Sprinkle remaining ½ cup Cheddar cheese over top. Bake at 350° for 30 minutes. Yields 4–6 servings.

Narice Sutton, Birmingham Life Club (Book 4)

Goulash

1 pound ground chuck
½ medium onion, chopped
½ medium bell pepper,
  chopped

1 (14½-ounce) can diced
  tomatoes
1 cup macaroni noodles, cooked
Salt and pepper to taste

Brown ground chuck with onion and bell pepper in a skillet, stirring until ground chuck is crumbly; drain. Stir in tomatoes and macaroni. Simmer 30 minutes, adding additional liquid as needed. Season with salt and pepper. Yields 4 servings.

Hazel Campbell, Birmingham Life Club (Book 4)

Hungarian Goulash

1 pound bulk sausage
2 (16-ounce) cans kidney beans
1 large onion, chopped
1 or 2 (14½ -ounce) cans diced
  tomatoes (or tomato juice)
1 teaspoon garlic salt

1½ teaspoons seasoning salt
1 teaspoon thyme
1 large bay leaf
1 quart water
1 large bell pepper, chopped
1 cup diced potatoes

Brown sausage; drain. Add beans, onion, tomatoes or juice, garlic salt, seasoning salt, thyme, bay leaf, and water. Simmer 45 minutes to an hour. Add bell pepper and potatoes. Turn up heat and cook until potatoes are done.

Note: For larger servings, use 2 pounds sausage and 3 cans kidney beans.

Janice A. McKinney, Birmingham South Council (Book 1)

Beef Stroganoff

½ stick butter or margarine
½ cup chopped onion
1½ pounds ground chuck
1 teaspoon salt
½ teaspoon black pepper
3 tablespoons all-purpose
   flour
1 (8-ounce) can water chestnuts,
   drained, thinly sliced

1 (4-ounce) can sliced
   mushrooms, undrained
1 (10¾-ounce) can cream of
   mushroom soup
1 cup sour cream
Cooked rice or Chinese noodles

Melt butter in skillet; add onion and sauté until transparent, but not brown. Add meat and brown. Stir in salt, pepper, and flour; blend well. Add water chestnuts, mushrooms with liquid, and soup. Cook and stir 5 minutes. Turn off heat and add sour cream. Serve over rice or Chinese noodles.

Sara P. Mitchell, Montgomery Council (Book 1)

Enchilada Pie

2 pounds ground chuck
1 medium onion, chopped
½ teaspoon salt
1 (10¾-ounce) can tomato soup
2 (10-ounce) cans mild
  enchilada sauce

1 cup water
12 or more (8-inch) tortilla
  shells
2 cups shredded cheese,
  divided

Brown ground chuck with onion and salt in a Dutch oven or large saucepan, stirring until ground chuck is crumbly; drain. Add soup, enchilada sauce, and water, and mix well. Simmer 5 minutes. Spoon ¾ of the ground chuck mixture into a bowl. Arrange 2 or 3 tortillas over remaining ground chuck mixture in the Dutch oven. Sprinkle with ¼ of the cheese. Repeat ground chuck mixture, tortilla, and cheese layers 3 more times. Simmer, covered, 10 minutes or until cheese melts and tortillas soften. Yields about 10 servings.

Gloria "Carol" Lindley,
Birmingham South Cahaba Council (Book 4)

Sloppy Joes

1 tablespoon oil
1 pound ground beef
1 large onion, finely chopped
½ green bell pepper, finely
  chopped
1 cup finely chopped celery
½ cup water

½ cup ketchup
⅛ cup cider vinegar
1 teaspoon salt
1 teaspoon chili powder
½ teaspoon pepper
½ teaspoon dry mustard
1 teaspoon Worcestershire

Place oil in a skillet, then add ground beef. Cook until brown, stirring with a fork. Add onion, green pepper, celery, and water. Cook over low heat until tender. Combine ketchup, vinegar, salt, chili powder, pepper, dry mustard, and Worcestershire sauce. Mix with browned meat mixture. Heat 5 minutes to blend flavors. Serve hot with toasted buns or fill soft hamburger buns with meat mixture. Wrap each bun separately in wax paper. Place on cookie sheet. Heat in a slow 325° oven for 20 minutes (optional). Makes 6–8 servings.

Janet Logsdon, Birmingham Central Council (Book 2)

Porcupine Meatballs

2 pounds hamburger meat
1½ cups rice, uncooked
1 medium onion, chopped
1 egg
½ teaspoon salt

Pepper to taste
½ teaspoon garlic salt
1 (14½-ounce) can tomatoes
1 (6-ounce) can tomato paste

Combine all ingredients except tomatoes and tomato paste; shape into small meatballs and place in pressure cooker. Add tomatoes and tomato paste; fill with water till meatballs are covered. Cook at 10 pounds pressure approximately 40–45 minutes.

Bea Windham, Montgomery Council (Book 1)

Spaghetti and Meatballs

MEATBALLS:

1 cup bread crumbs
4 or 5 eggs
1 tablespoon parsley
2 pounds ground chuck
1 pound lean ground pork
½ onion, finely chopped

2 pods garlic, chopped very fine
2 teaspoons Italian cheese
  (Romano or Parmesan)
Salt and pepper to taste
Oil for frying

Mix bread crumbs, eggs, and parsley together; add remaining ingredients except oil. Mix thoroughly; if mixture feels dry, you may add a little milk. Mixture should be workable. Roll into balls; fry in oil about 10 minutes.

SPAGHETTI SAUCE:

1 large onion, chopped
2 or 3 pods garlic, finely
  chopped
6 (12-ounce) cans tomato paste
4 (15-ounce) cans tomato sauce
10 (12-ounce) cans water
1 tablespoon chopped parsley
Pinch of rosemary

1 tablespoon chopped sweet
  basil
1 bay leaf
1 cup sugar (more or less to
  taste)
Salt and pepper to taste
Cooked spaghetti noodles

Fry onion and garlic in same grease that you used for frying meatballs. Pour tomato paste and sauce into a large pot; add water, garlic, onion, and remaining ingredients. Let sauce cook 1 hour, then put meatballs in. The sauce has to cook on medium to low heat for at least 4½–5 hours. Stir often to keep from sticking; the longer it cooks, the better it gets. Remove bay leaf before serving. Serve over cooked spaghetti noodles.

Rosemary Parker, Birmingham Central Council (Book 2)

Beef Roast with Gravy

1 (2- to 3-pound) beef roast
1 (10¾-ounce) can cream of
  mushroom soup

½ cup water
½ envelope onion soup mix

Rinse roast and pat dry; place in deep roasting pan. Spread with mixture of mushroom soup and water; sprinkle with onion soup mix. Roast, tightly covered with foil, at 350° for 1½–2 hours or until very tender, adding water if needed during roasting time. Serve with mashed potatoes or rice. May use inexpensive cuts of beef for this recipe. Yields 6 servings.

Maxine Pinckard (Mrs. Ken Pinckard), Montgomery Council
(Book 3)

Best-Ever Pot Roast

1 (3-pound) chuck roast
4 garlic cloves
Salt and pepper to taste
Flour for coating
2 tablespoons olive oil
1½ cups cooking wine
¾ cup brewed coffee

2 envelopes onion and
  mushroom soup mix
5 carrots, cut into 1-inch pieces
4 ribs celery, cut into 1-inch
  pieces
1 large onion, coarsely chopped
4 or 5 potatoes, cut into halves

Cut 4 slits in sides of roast and insert garlic cloves. Sprinkle with salt and pepper. Coat lightly with flour. Brown roast in hot oil in a Dutch oven. Combine wine, coffee, and soup mix in a bowl; mix well. Pour over roast. Bake at 350° for 1 hour. Add carrots, celery, and onion. Bake for 1 hour more. Add potatoes; bake an additional hour. Place vegetables in serving bowl. Place roast on serving plate and cut into slices. Pour gravy into a bowl. Yields 8–10 servings.

Margie Stetson, Riverchase Council (Book 4)

Veal Parmigiana

2 pounds boneless veal cutlets
⅓ cup olive oil
¼ pound sliced fresh
  mushrooms
½ cup freshly grated Parmesan
  cheese
1¼ cups crumbled bread
  crumbs

1 tablespoon water
2 eggs, beaten
2 (8-ounce) cans tomato sauce
1 teaspoon salt
¼ teaspoon pepper
½ teaspoon rosemary
3 ounces sliced mozzarella
  cheese

With a meat hammer, pound veal until extremely thin. Cut into 6 equal pieces. Heat olive oil and sauté mushrooms. Remove from oil. Mix together Parmesan and bread crumbs. Place water, eggs, salt and pepper to taste in a bowl; mix well. Dip veal first in egg mixture and then in breadcrumbs. Brown cutlets in olive oil, then add tomato sauce, seasonings, mushrooms, and sliced mozzarella over veal. Reduce heat; cover and allow to simmer 10–20 minutes. Remove from heat and serve.

Brenda Stewart, Decatur Council (Book 1)

 Emma M. Nutt was the first female employee for the Bell Telephone Company. She was hired at the Boston exchange September 1, 1878, and continued until her retirement in 1915. Her 37 years as an operator began a tradition of long service.

Country Fried Steak

1 pound ground beef
3 tablespoons plus 1 teaspoon
  all-purpose flour
1 teaspoon Ac'cent

2 tablespoons dry milk
2 tablespoons Worcestershire
Salt and pepper to taste
Oil for frying

Combine all ingredients. Make into patties and roll in additional flour. Brown on both sides in hot oil. Place in a casserole dish. If desired, make gravy in some of the oil the steak was browned in; add a bouillon cube to the gravy. Pour gravy over steak and bake for 30 minutes in a 330° oven.

Vivian Wilder, Anniston Council (Book 2)

Ms. Kay's Chinese Steak

1½ pounds sirloin steak
1 clove garlic, crushed
1 teaspoon salt
½ teaspoon pepper
¼ cup vegetable oil
3 green bell peppers, sliced
2 onions, sliced

1 (7-ounce) can sliced water
  chestnuts, drained
¼ cup soy sauce
½ teaspoon sugar
1 (10-ounce) can beef consommé
2 tablespoons cornstarch
¼ cup water

Slice steak into ⅛-inch strips. Stir-fry garlic with salt and pepper in heated oil in skillet. Add steak. Stir-fry until light brown; remove to bowl. Add green peppers and onions to skillet. Stir-fry 3–5 minutes or until tender. Return steak to skillet. Add water chestnuts, soy sauce, sugar, and beef consommé. Stir in mixture of cornstarch and water. Simmer 5 minutes or until thickened, stirring constantly. Serve over rice. Garnish with green onions. Yields 6 servings.

Sheila Brothers, Anniston Council (Book 3)

Corned Beef Casserole

1 (12-ounce) can corned beef,
  crumbled
¼ pound chopped American
  cheese
1 (10¾-ounce) can cream of
  chicken soup

1 cup milk
½ cup chopped onion
1 (8-ounce) package noodles,
  cooked, drained
¾ cup buttered bread crumbs

Combine all ingredients except noodles and bread crumbs.
Alternate layers of meat mixture with noodles in greased 2-quart
casserole; top with bread crumbs and bake 30 minutes in 375°
oven.

Jamima Edney, Birmingham South Council (Book 1)

Corned Beef and Cabbage Casserole

3 large white potatoes
1 large onion
½ stick margarine
Salt and pepper to taste
½ head (about) green cabbage,
  chopped

1 (12-ounce) can corned beef
1 (10¾-ounce) can cream of
  mushroom soup
1–1½ cups shredded mild or
  medium Cheddar cheese

Peel and slice potatoes. Arrange in a layer over bottom of a 9x13-
inch baking pan sprayed with nonstick cooking spray. Peel and
slice onion. Arrange in layer over potatoes. Dot with margarine.
Sprinkle with salt and pepper. Arrange cabbage over layers.
Spread corned beef over cabbage. Spread soup over corned beef.
Sprinkle cheese over top. Cover with foil sprayed with nonstick
cooking spray. Bake at 375° for 1 hour. Yields 4–6 servings.

Bertha Capps, Birmingham Life Club (Book 4)

Corned Beef Squares and Cabbage

2 (12-ounce) cans corned beef, crumbled
1 cup milk
1 cup cracker crumbs
2 eggs, beaten
½ cup coarsely chopped onion
1 tablespoon horseradish
1 teaspoon prepared mustard
1 medium head cabbage
1 (10¾-ounce) can cream of mushroom soup, undiluted
⅔ cup milk
1 teaspoon dill seeds
1 teaspoon mustard seeds

Combine first 7 ingredients; mix well. Spoon into a greased 9-inch-square pan; bake at 350° for 30 minutes.

Cut cabbage into 9 wedges; cover and cook 10 minutes in a small amount of boiling, salted water. Drain cabbage well.

Combine soup, milk, dill seeds, and mustard seeds in a small saucepan; cook over medium heat, stirring constantly, until mixture comes to a boil. Remove from heat.

Cut corned beef mixture into 9 squares. Carefully arrange the cabbage wedges and corned beef squares on a serving platter, then pour soup mixture over top. Yields 9 servings.

Regina Cash, Anniston Council (Book 1)

Spicy Sausage Casserole

½ pound hot or mild bulk
  sausage
¼ cup chopped green bell
  pepper
¼ cup chopped onion
1 (14½-ounce) can diced
  tomatoes, undrained
¾ can water

1 cup uncooked macaroni
  (seashell or other)
⅛ teaspoon Italian seasoning
½ teaspoon salt
⅛ teaspoon pepper
Dash of chili powder
½ cup shredded Cheddar
  cheese

Brown sausage in skillet; pour off drippings. Reduce heat; add pepper, onion, tomatoes, water, macaroni, and seasonings. Cover and simmer 25 minutes; uncover and simmer 10 minutes. Spoon into a lightly greased 1-quart casserole. Sprinkle with cheese. Place in 325° oven till cheese has melted.

Hazel Campbell, Birmingham South Council (Book 1)

Johnson's Sausage Dressing

1 pound bulk sausage
1 large onion, chopped
2 ribs celery, chopped
1 stick margarine
2½ cups crumbled cornbread

2½ cups crumbled biscuits
1 teaspoon salt
¼ teaspoon pepper
1 tablespoon poultry seasoning
2 (14-ounce) cans chicken broth

Brown sausage in a skillet, stirring until crumbly; drain. Cook onion and celery in margarine in a separate skillet until tender. Combine cornbread, biscuits, salt, pepper, and poultry seasoning in a large bowl; mix well. Add broth, onion mixture, and cooked sausage; mix well. Spoon into a large greased baking dish. Bake at 350° for 30–35 minutes. Yields 6–8 servings.

James B. Johnson, Jr., Tuscaloosa Council (Book 4)

Garlic-Mustard Pork Chops

3 tablespoons olive oil
2 tablespoons Dijon mustard
5 cloves garlic, minced
3 tablespoons chopped parsley

2 teaspoons thyme
½ teaspoon pepper
4 (¾-inch-thick) center-cut pork
 chops

Combine olive oil, mustard, garlic, parsley, thyme, and pepper in shallow dish; mix well. Add pork chops, turning to coat well. Marinate, covered, in refrigerator 6 hours or longer, turning occasionally. Let chops stand until room temperature. Heat cast-iron skillet over medium-high heat 3 minutes or until very hot. Add chops. Cook 4–5 minutes or until brown on bottom. Turn chops. Cook 4–5 minutes longer or until cooked through. Yields 4 servings.

Brenda B. Reeves, Birmingham South Council (Book 3)

Crockpot Pork Chops

8–10 pork chops
Salt and pepper to taste
2 cups flour
¼ cup water
2 (10¾-ounce) cans cream of
 celery soup

1 (10¾-ounce) can Cheddar
 cheese soup
1 onion, chopped
½ cup chopped celery
¼ cup chopped bell pepper
1 cup shredded Cheddar cheese

Season pork chops with salt and pepper. Coat with flour. Brown in oil on both sides in a skillet. Arrange ½ the pork chops over bottom of crockpot. Pour water over pork chops. Layer ½ the celery soup, ½ the cheese soup, ½ onion, ½ celery, and ½ the bell pepper over pork chops. Arrange remaining pork chops over layers. Layer remaining soups, onion, celery, and bell pepper over pork chops. Sprinkle cheese over top. Cook on HIGH 5–6 hours or on LOW 8–12 hours. Serve over rice. Yields 8–10 servings.

Barbara Seegmiller, Decatur Council (Book 4)

Apple-Crumb Stuffed Pork Chops

APPLE-CRUMB STUFFING:

1 cup soft bread crumbs
½ cup diced apple
3 tablespoons minced onion
3 tablespoons chopped raisins
½ teaspoon salt

½ teaspoon sugar
Pinch of pepper
Pinch of ground sage
1½ tablespoons butter or
  margarine, melted

Combine all ingredients; mix well. Yields about 1¾ cups.

PORK CHOPS:

4 (1-inch-thick) pork chops, cut
  with pockets
Salt and pepper to taste

1 tablespoon butter or
  margarine
3 tablespoons water

Stuff pockets of pork chops with Apple-Crumb Stuffing and secure with toothpicks. Sprinkle pork chops with salt and pepper. Melt butter in a large heavy skillet; brown pork chops on both sides. Add water; reduce heat. Cover and simmer 50–55 minutes or until pork chops are tender. Yields 4 servings.

Faith Kirby, Anniston Council (Book 1)

Mandarin Pork Chops

4 (4-ounce) center-cut
  pork chops
1 tablespoon vegetable oil
½ cup orange juice
¼ cup water
3 tablespoons brown sugar
2 tablespoons lemon juice

1 tablespoon cornstarch
2 teaspoons chicken bouillon
  granules
1 (11-ounce) can Mandarin
  oranges, drained
1 medium green bell pepper,
  sliced

Brown pork chops on both sides in oil in a skillet. Remove from skillet and set aside. Add orange juice, water, brown sugar, lemon juice, cornstarch, and bouillon to skillet. Cook until thickened, stirring constantly. Add pork chops. Simmer, covered, 20 minutes or until pork chops are tender and cooked through. Add oranges and bell pepper. Cook until heated through. Yields 4 servings.

Hazel E. Campbell, Birmingham Life Club (Book 4)

Ham (or Spam) Casserole

1 small green bell pepper,
  chopped
1 medium onion, chopped
¼ cup margarine
1–1½ cups chopped bite-size
  ham, or 1 can Spam, chopped
  bite-size

1 (15-ounce) can whole-kernel
  corn
2 tablespoons flour
1½ cups milk
Salt and pepper to taste
1 package or box cornbread mix

Simmer chopped green pepper and onion in margarine; add ham or Spam and corn. Sprinkle flour over these ingredients. Add milk; stir and cook until slightly thickened. Salt and pepper to taste. Mix cornbread mix as directed on package or box. Drop in large tablespoons over top of mixture; bake in 400° oven until bread is done according to package directions, approximately 15–20 minutes.

Beverly McCoy, Montgomery Council (Book 1)

Quick Ham-Broccoli Casserole

¼ cup chopped onion
1 (10-ounce) package frozen
   chopped broccoli, thawed,
   drained
2 tablespoons butter or
   margarine, melted
1 (10¾-ounce) can cream of
   chicken soup, undiluted

2 cups chopped, cooked ham
1 cup uncooked instant rice
½ cup processed cheese spread
¼ cup milk
½ teaspoon Worcestershire

Sauté onion and broccoli in butter in a large skillet until onion is tender. Remove from heat; stir in remaining ingredients. Spoon mixture into a lightly greased 1½-quart casserole. Bake at 350° for 25–30 minutes or until bubbly. Yields 6 servings.

Regina Cash, Anniston Council (Book 1)

Chunky Ham Casserole

1 (7-ounce) package elbow
   macaroni
1 (10¾-ounce) can cream of
   mushroom soup
⅔ cup evaporated milk
4 ounces shredded Cheddar
   cheese (1 cup)

Salt to taste
1 (4-ounce) can sliced
   mushrooms
6 ounces canned or fresh
   ham, chunked
½ cup cracker crumbs

Prepare macaroni according to package directions; drain. Mix together soup, milk, cheese, salt, mushrooms, and ham; add macaroni and mix well. Pour into buttered 2-quart baking dish. Top with cracker crumbs. Bake, uncovered, for 45 minutes or until bubbly at 350°. Serves 4.

Rita Moore, Anniston Council (Book 1)

Grilled Ham Steak

¼ cup apricot or plum
  preserves
1 tablespoon prepared mustard
1 teaspoon lemon juice

⅛ teaspoon cinnamon
1 (2-pound, 1-inch-thick) ham
  steak

Combine preserves, mustard, lemon juice, and cinnamon in a saucepan. Cook over medium heat 2–3 minutes, stirring constantly. Score fat edge of ham. Grill over medium-hot coals 8–10 minutes per side, brushing with preserve mixture during last 5 minutes. Yields 6 servings.

Alice Walski, Birmingham Life Club (Book 4)

Tangy Barbecued Spareribs

3 pounds spareribs
1 large onion, finely chopped
2 cloves garlic, finely chopped
2 tablespoons vegetable oil
1 (12-ounce) bottle chili sauce

½ cup lemon juice
¼ cup molasses
¼ cup dark rum
3 tablespoons Dijon mustard
1 tablespoon Worcestershire

Cut ribs into serving-size pieces (3–4 ribs per person); place in a large Dutch oven. Add enough water to cover ribs; cover and simmer 40 minutes. Drain ribs, and place in a shallow baking dish. Set ribs aside.

Sauté onion and garlic in oil in a medium saucepan until onion is tender. Stir in remaining ingredients; reduce heat and simmer 25 minutes. Pour barbecue sauce over ribs; cover and marinate overnight in refrigerator.

Place ribs, bone side down, on grill over slow coals. Grill 20 minutes; turn meat side down, and cook 10–15 minutes. Brush ribs with sauce, and let cook 5–10 additional minutes on each side. Yields 4–5 servings.

Regina Cash, Anniston Council (Book 1)

Barbecue Sauce for Spareribs, Steaks, and Hamburgers

2 tablespoons butter
1 medium onion, sliced
1 clove garlic, minced
½ cup chopped celery
¾ cup water
1 cup ketchup
2 tablespoons vinegar

2 tablespoons lemon juice
2 tablespoons Worcestershire
2 tablespoons brown sugar
1 teaspoon dry mustard
1 teaspoon salt
¼ teaspoon pepper

Melt butter; add onion and cook until lightly browned. Add remaining ingredients and cook 20 minutes. Makes about 2¼ cups, or enough for 3 pounds of meat.

Berniece Peterson, Birmingham South Council (Book 1)

Grilled Stuffed Franks

1 (8-ounce) can tomato sauce
1 tablespoon sugar
2 tablespoons spicy brown
  mustard
½ teaspoon garlic powder

8 frankfurters
6 small green onions, chopped
8 slices bacon
8 hot dog buns

Combine tomato sauce, sugar, mustard, and garlic powder; stir well. Slice frankfurters lengthwise to make a pocket. Brush inside each pocket with sauce; sprinkle with onion. Wrap each frankfurter with bacon, securing with a wooden pick. Cook frankfurters over hot coals 10–15 minutes or until bacon is crisp, turning often and basting with remaining sauce. Serve in hot dog buns. Yields 8 servings.

Regina Cash, Anniston Council (Book 1)

Poultry

1954
"500" Series

With the invention of the transistor in 1947, the vacuum tube transmitter was soon replaced. Equipment size was reduced and reliability increased, making telephone service more affordable. The telephone started to become a decorative household item in the early 1950s. Although some colored telephones were available much earlier, they did not gain widespread popularity until the advent of the "500" color series. Besides black, the five basic colors available were white, beige, green, pink, and blue. Standard with all the sets was an adjustable volume control for the bell. An improved, more flexible neoprene jacketed telephone cord replaced the cotton covered cords used since telephony began. As many households began using more than one phone, the telephone returned to the wall in a companion piece to the "500" desk set. The wall set was most often used in the kitchen where counter and table space was at a premium.

Apricot Chicken

4 chicken breast fillets
2 tablespoons butter
1 medium onion, chopped
½ cup chopped green bell
   pepper
1 tablespoon all-purpose flour
1 tablespoon paprika
1 teaspoon salt
¼ teaspoon white pepper
2 cups chicken broth
1 cup sour cream
¼ teaspoon grated lemon rind
½ cup finely chopped dried
   apricots
2 cups hot cooked egg noodles

Rinse chicken fillets and pat dry. Sauté chicken in butter in skillet until brown. Arrange chicken in greased 7x11-inch baking dish. Add onion and green pepper to pan drippings. Cook until vegetables are tender, stirring constantly. Add flour, paprika, salt, and white pepper; mix well. Stir in chicken broth gradually. Cook until thickened, stirring constantly. Remove from heat. Stir in sour cream, lemon rind, and apricots. Pour sauce over chicken. Bake at 350° for 20–30 minutes or until chicken is tender. Place noodles on serving platter. Arrange chicken over noodles; top with sauce. Yields 4 servings.

Verlan Harden, Phenix City Club (Book 3)

Drunk Chicken

1 (3-pound) chicken
Cajun seasoning, or your favorite
   seasoning, to taste
1 (12-ounce) can beer

Sprinkle outside surface of chicken with seasoning. Sit chicken upright on open can of beer. Cook in a smoker 3½ hours. Be careful when removing chicken from smoker. Use a spatula under the can of beer to help remove chicken. Yields 4 servings.

Sara Cooley, Birmingham Life Club (Book 4)

Copycat Kentucky Fried Chicken

3 pounds chicken parts
¼ cup lemon juice
1½ cups baking mix
2 envelopes Italian salad
  dressing mix
3 tablespoons flour
2 teaspoons salt

1 teaspoon paprika
½ teaspoon sage
¼ teaspoon pepper
1 cup milk
2 tablespoons butter, melted
Vegetable oil for frying

Combine chicken and lemon juice in a bowl and toss to coat. Marinate, covered, in refrigerator for 30–60 minutes; drain.

Combine baking mix, salad dressing mix, flour, salt, paprika, sage, and pepper in a shallow dish; mix well. Whisk milk and butter in a bowl until blended. Dip chicken in milk mixture and coat with flour mixture. Fry chicken in oil in a skillet until brown on both sides; drain. Arrange on baking sheet. Bake at 350° until cooked through and crispy. Yields 5 servings.

Barbara Seegmiller, Decatur Council (Book 4)

Detroit, Michigan, was the first city in the nation to assign individual telephone numbers in 1879.

Pan-Fried Chicken

4 boneless skinless chicken
  breasts
1 cup dry bread crumbs
½ teaspoon garlic powder

⅛ teaspoon light salt
1 tablespoons vegetable oil,
  divided

Pound chicken lightly between sheets of wax paper. Mix bread crumbs, garlic powder, and salt in a shallow dish. Coat chicken with crumb mixture. Let stand several minutes to allow coating to adhere. Spray a skillet with nonstick cooking spray. Heat over medium heat until hot. Add 1½ teaspoons oil, tilting skillet to coat bottom. Add chicken. Pan-fry until brown on one side. Add remaining 1½ teaspoons oil. Turn chicken; pan-fry until cooked through. Yields 4 servings.

Gloria "Carol" Lindley, Birmingham South Cahaba Council
(Book 4)

Alma's Baked Chicken

3 tablespoons flour
½ teaspoon seasoned salt
½ teaspoon garlic salt

½ teaspoon paprika
⅓ cup margarine, melted
6 chicken breasts, skinned

Combine flour, seasoned salt, garlic salt, and paprika in a bowl and mix well. Stir in margarine. Coat chicken with flour mixture. Arrange chicken in a single layer in a baking pan lined with foil. Bake at 450° for 20 minutes. Reduce oven temperature to 350°. Bake 1 hour longer or until cooked through. Yields 6 servings.

Marie Hartley, Birmingham South Life Club (Book 4)

Zippy Chicken Stir-Fry

½ cup Miracle Whip
1 tablespoon soy sauce
½ teaspoon ginger
¼ teaspoon red pepper flakes
  (optional)
2 tablespoons vegetable oil
3 boneless skinless chicken
  breasts, cut into thin strips

1 cup broccoli florets
1 cup julienne red bell pepper
1 cup carrot sticks
¼ cup sliced green onions
1 garlic clove, minced
4 cups hot cooked rice

Combine Miracle Whip, soy sauce, ginger, and red pepper flakes in a bowl; mix well. Heat oil in a wok or large skillet over medium-high heat until hot. Add chicken. Stir-fry 4 minutes; add broccoli, bell pepper, carrots, green onions, and garlic. Stir-fry 3–4 minutes or until vegetables are tender-crisp. Stir in salad dressing mixture. Simmer 30 seconds, stirring constantly. Spoon over rice on a serving platter. Yields 3–4 servings.

Mary Alice Neal, Birmingham Life Club (Book 4)

Sticky Chicken

1 cup packed brown sugar
¾ cup soy sauce
½ cup teriyaki sauce
1 stick butter or margarine,
  melted

1 tablespoon Creole seasoning
1 teaspoon dry mustard
2 pounds chicken wings

Combine brown sugar, soy sauce, teriyaki sauce, butter, Creole seasoning, and dry mustard in a bowl and mix well. Pour over chicken in a sealable plastic bag; seal tightly. Turn to coat. Marinate in refrigerator 1–10 hours, turning occasionally; drain.

Arrange chicken in baking pan. Bake at 375° for 1 hour.

Frankie Vaughn, Selma Life Club (Book 4)

Sesame Chicken Kabobs

2 whole chicken breasts,
  skinned, boned
¼ cup soy sauce
¼ cup reduced-calorie Russian
  salad dressing
1 tablespoon sesame seeds
2 tablespoons lemon juice
¼ teaspoon ground ginger
¼ teaspoon garlic powder

1 large green bell pepper, cut
  into 1-inch pieces
2 medium onions, cut into
  eighths
3 small zucchini, cut into
  ¾-inch pieces
1 pint cherry tomatoes
Vegetable cooking spray

Cut chicken breasts into 1-inch pieces; place chicken in a shallow container, and set aside. Combine next 6 ingredients in a jar; cover tightly and shake vigorously. Pour over chicken; cover and marinate in refrigerator at least 2 hours.

Remove chicken from marinade, reserving marinade. Alternate chicken and vegetables on skewers. Spray grill with cooking spray. Grill kabobs about 6 inches from medium-hot coals for 15–20 minutes or until done, turning and basting often with marinade. Yields 6 servings.

Regina Cash, Anniston Council (Book 1)

Light and Sticky Chicken

⅓ cup honey
¼ cup prepared mustard
2 tablespoons butter
1 teaspoon curry powder

¼ teaspoon salt
4 (8-ounce) chicken breasts,
  skinned

Combine first 5 ingredients in a saucepan. Cook over low heat until blended, stirring frequently. Place chicken in a sealable plastic bag. Pour honey mixture over chicken and seal tightly. Turn to coat. Marinate in refrigerator 2–10 hours, turning occasionally.

Arrange undrained chicken in a single layer in a 9x13-inch baking pan sprayed with nonstick cooking spray. Bake at 400° for 30–40 minutes, or until chicken is cooked through, basting with pan juices 3 times. Yields 4 servings.

Mary C. Martin, Birmingham Life Club (Book 4)

Crunchy Chicken Casserole

3 cups chopped, cooked
  chicken
½ cup slivered almonds
1 (8½-ounce) can water
  chestnuts, thinly sliced
¼ cup chopped pimiento
¼ teaspoon celery salt
⅛ teaspoon pepper

⅛ teaspoon paprika
1 tablespoon chopped parsley
1 (10¾-ounce) can cream of
  mushroom soup
½ cup French-fried onion rings,
  crumbled
½ cup shredded sharp Cheddar
  cheese

Combine all ingredients except onion rings and cheese; pour into a greased 1½-quart casserole. Sprinkle onion rings and cheese over top; bake at 350° for 30 minutes. Yields 6 servings.

Faith Kirby, Anniston Council (Book 1)

Poppy Seed Chicken Casserole

1 (3-pound) chicken, cooked,
    drained
1 (10¾-ounce) can cream of
    chicken soup
1 (10¾-ounce) can cream of
    mushroom soup

1 cup sour cream
¼ cup poppy seeds
2 envelopes ranch salad dressing
    mix
65 butter crackers, crushed
1 stick butter, melted

Chop chicken, discarding skin and bones. Combine chicken, soups, sour cream, poppy seeds, and dressing mix in a large bowl; mix well. Spoon into a baking dish sprayed with nonstick cooking spray. Combine cracker crumbs and butter in a bowl; mix well. Sprinkle over chicken mixture. Bake at 375° for 35 minutes. Yields 8 servings.

Lynn Sherrer, Montgomery Council (Book 4)

Chicken Pie

1 (3-pound) chicken
1 (15-ounce) can mixed
    vegetables, drained
2 (10¾-ounce) cans cream of
    chicken soup

1 (14-ounce) can chicken broth
1 All Ready Pie Pastry

Rinse chicken and pat dry. Bake chicken in slow cooker or oven cooking bag until tender. Chop chicken, discarding skin and bones. Spoon mixed vegetables into baking dish. Top with chicken. Spoon mixture of soup and broth over chicken. Top with pastry. Crimp edges to seal; cut vents. Bake at 375° for 25–30 minutes, or until brown. Yields 8 servings.

Virginia H. Greene, Birmingham Life Club (Book 3)

Biscuit-Topped Chicken Pie

1 (4-pound) chicken, cut up
1 tablespoon salt
2 stalks celery
1 bay leaf
1 onion, cut in quarters
7 tablespoons margarine
7 tablespoons flour

1 cup light cream
2 cups chicken broth
Salt and pepper to taste
Mace to taste
½ teaspoon Worcestershire
1 (10-count) can biscuits

Rinse chicken. Combine chicken, salt, celery, bay leaf, onion, and enough water to cover in stockpot. Simmer until chicken is tender; drain. Chop chicken, discarding skin and bones. Arrange in 2-quart baking dish. Melt margarine in double boiler over hot water. Stir in flour until smooth. Add cream and broth; mix well. Cook over boiling water until thickened, stirring constantly. Season with salt and pepper to taste, mace, and Worcestershire. Cook until bubbly, stirring constantly. Spoon into prepared baking dish. Roll biscuits to flatten; arrange over chicken mixture. Bake at 450° for 20–25 minutes or until biscuits are brown. Yields 8 servings.

Marie Boothe, Bon Secour Life Club (Book 3)

The coin-operated pay telephone was patented by William Gray of Hartford, Connecticut, in 1889.

Old-Fashioned Chicken Pie

1 (3-pound) chicken, cooked,
   boned, chopped
1 (10¾-ounce) can cream of
   chicken soup
½ cup water

Pepper to taste
1½ cups buttermilk
1½ cups self-rising flour
½ cup margarine, melted
2 cups chicken broth

Line bottom of baking dish with chicken. Spoon mixture of soup
and water over chicken; sprinkle with pepper. Top with mixture
of buttermilk, flour, and margarine. Pour broth over layers. Bake
at 350° for 1 hour or until brown. Yields 6 servings.

Imogene Davis, Birmingham Life Club (Book 3)

Chicken Pot Pie

1 (3-pound) chicken, cooked,
   drained
1 (16-ounce) can peas and
   carrots, drained
2 (10¾-ounce) cans cream of
   chicken soup

1 medium onion, chopped
1 (10¾-ounce) can cream of
   celery soup
1 cup flour
1 cup milk
¾ cup mayonnaise

Chop chicken, discarding skin and bones. Combine chicken, peas
and carrots, chicken soup, onion, and celery soup in a bowl; mix
gently. Spoon into a 9x13-inch baking pan sprayed with nonstick
cooking spray. Combine flour, milk, and mayonnaise in a bowl,
stirring until blended. Pour over chicken mixture. Bake at 350° for
1 hour. Yields 6–8 servings.

Margaret W. Wilborn, Gadsden Life Club (Book 4)

Easy Chicken and Rice

4–6 boneless chicken breasts
2 (10¾-ounce) cans cream of
  chicken soup

1 (10¾-ounce) can cream of
  mushroom soup
2 cups hot cooked rice

Rinse chicken and pat dry. Combine soups in a bowl; mix well. Spoon into baking dish. Press chicken into soup mixture, spooning some of mixture over chicken. Bake, covered, at 375° for 1 hour or until chicken is tender. Serve with rice. Yields 6 servings.

Janet Sandlin, Birmingham South Cahaba Council (Book 3)

Low-Fat Quick Chicken Cacciatore

3 pounds chicken breast fillets
¼ cup vegetable oil
1¾ cups water
1 (12-ounce) can tomato paste
1 envelope spaghetti sauce mix
¼ cup onion flakes

1 (4-ounce) can mushroom
  pieces
3 cups rice, cooked
½ cup slivered almonds, toasted
  (optional)

Rinse chicken and pat dry. Sauté chicken in oil in skillet until brown on all sides. Remove to platter. Add water, tomato paste, sauce mix, and onion flakes to pan drippings; mix well. Return chicken to skillet. Simmer, covered, for 40 minutes or until chicken is tender. Stir in mushrooms just before serving. Place chicken on serving platter. Surround with rice; sprinkle with almonds, if desired. Yields 12 servings.

Charlie Mae Hickman, Phenix City Club (Book 3)

Cornbread Casserole

4–6 skinless, boneless chicken breasts

1 (8- or 9-inch) pan cornbread, cooked

1 stick margarine, melted

1 (10¾-ounce) can cream of celery soup

1 (10¾-ounce) can cream of chicken soup

1 cup chicken broth (from boiling chicken breasts)

2 boiled eggs, sliced

Boil chicken breasts until done; save 1 cup broth. Cut chicken into bite-size pieces; set aside. Crumble cornbread until fine; pour melted margarine over cornbread. Mix well; set aside. To meat, add both cans soup and reserved chicken broth; mix well.

In bottom of 9x13-inch baking dish, put a little more than half the cornbread, then spoon on meat mixture. Top with sliced eggs and remaining crumbled cornbread. Bake at 325° till bubbly.

Agnes Trott, Montgomery Council (Book 1)

Chicken and Broccoli Casserole

2 whole chicken breasts and 6 thighs, cooked, diced

2 (10-ounce) packages chopped broccoli, cooked

2 (10¾-ounce) cans cream of chicken soup

1 cup mayonnaise

1 tablespoon lemon juice

1 teaspoon curry powder

1 package Pepperidge Farm Herb Dressing

1 stick butter or margarine, melted

Place diced chicken in 3-quart shallow casserole dish; top with broccoli. Mix soup, mayonnaise, lemon juice, and curry powder. Pour over chicken and broccoli. Sprinkle herb dressing over top. Pour melted butter over all. Cover lightly with aluminum foil to keep topping from browning too rapidly. Bake at 350° for 30 minutes. Serves 12.

Rochelle Yarbrough, Montgomery Council (Book 1)

Liz's Chicken and Dressing

4 chicken leg quarters, cooked
1 (9-inch) skillet cornbread,
  crumbled
1 large onion, chopped
1 large green bell pepper,
  chopped

1 cup chopped celery
1½ cups chicken broth, divided
Sage to taste
Salt and pepper to taste

Chop chicken, discarding skin and bones. Combine chicken and cornbread in a bowl; mix well. Sauté onion, bell pepper, and celery in 1 cup broth in a skillet. Add chicken mixture; mix well. Gradually stir in remaining ½ cup broth, sage, salt and pepper, stirring until of desired consistency. Spoon into baking pan. Bake at 365° for 45 minutes or until brown and bubbly. Yields 4–6 servings.

Elizabeth S. Hatcher, Riverchase Council (Book 4)

Chicken Enchiladas

2 cups sour cream
1 (10¾-ounce) can cream of
  chicken soup
2 large chicken breasts,
  chopped or cut into strips

1 onion, julienne
Butter
1 large package tortillas
2 cups shredded mozzarella
  cheese

Combine sour cream and soup in a bowl; mix well. Sauté chicken and onion in butter in a skillet until chicken is cooked through. Add half the sour cream mixture; mix well. Simmer 10 minutes, stirring frequently. Spoon chicken mixture onto tortillas and roll to enclose filling. Arrange tortillas seam side down in a greased baking dish. Spread with remaining sour cream mixture. Bake at 350° for 15 minutes. Sprinkle with cheese. Bake just until cheese melts. Yields 8–10 servings.

Sally McCrorie, Riverchase Council (Book 4)

Chicken Salad Tacos

1 (10-ounce) can chunk white
  chicken, drained, flaked
⅓ cup salsa
¼ cup sour cream
1 rib celery, chopped
1 teaspoon cumin

8 taco shells
1 cup shredded iceberg lettuce
1 small tomato, chopped
½ cup shredded Cheddar
  cheese

Combine chicken, salsa, sour cream, celery, and cumin in a bowl; mix well. Spoon chicken mixture into taco shells. Top each taco with lettuce, tomato, and cheese. Serve immediately. Yields 8 servings.

Mary C. Martin, Birmingham Life Club (Book 4)

Chicken Fajitas

1 (5- to 6-ounce) chicken breast
  fillet, cut into strips
1 small onion, cut into thin
  strips
½ green bell pepper, cut
  into thin strips
½ cup oil

½ teaspoon salt
½ teaspoon garlic powder
1 teaspoon chili powder
2 flour tortillas
1 tablespoon sour cream
1 tablespoon salsa

Rinse chicken and pat dry. Combine chicken strips, onion, and green pepper in glass or plastic container. Pour mixture of oil, salt, garlic powder, and chili powder over chicken mixture, tossing to coat. Marinate, covered, in refrigerator overnight to 2 days. Drain, discarding marinade. Sauté chicken, onion, and green pepper in nonstick skillet until chicken is tender, stirring constantly. Microwave tortillas on HIGH for 10 seconds. Spread chicken mixture on tortillas; roll to enclose filling. Serve with sour cream and salsa. Serves 1.

Pattie Smith, Gadsden Life Club (Book 3)

Chicken Tetrazzini

1 medium onion, chopped
¼ cup chopped celery
3 tablespoons butter
2 cups diced cooked chicken
6 ounces spaghetti, uncooked, broken in pieces
1 (10¾-ounce) can cream of chicken soup, undiluted
2½ cups chicken broth or bouillon
1 teaspoon lemon juice
¼ teaspoon pepper
Pinch of nutmeg
1 (4-ounce) can sliced mushrooms, drained
Grated Parmesan and paprika

Sauté onion and celery in butter in Dutch oven until crisp-tender. Arrange chicken in layer over vegetables; add spaghetti in layer. Combine soup, broth, lemon juice, pepper, and nutmeg, and pour over spaghetti, making certain all spaghetti is moistened. Sprinkle mushrooms over top. Cover and bring to a boil; reduce heat and simmer, stirring constantly, 15–20 minutes, until spaghetti is tender. Garnish with Parmesan cheese and paprika.

N. Shanks, Anniston Council (Book 1)

Chicken and Dumpling Casserole

½ cup chopped onion
½ cup chopped celery
2 garlic cloves, minced
½ stick butter or margarine
½ cup flour
2 teaspoons sugar
1 teaspoon salt
3 teaspoons basil, divided

½ teaspoon pepper
4 cups chicken broth
1 (10-ounce) package frozen
  green peas
4 cups chopped cooked chicken
2 cups baking mix
2 teaspoons basil
⅔ cup milk

Sauté onion, celery, and garlic in butter in a saucepan until vegetables are tender. Stir in flour, sugar, salt, 1 teaspoon basil, and pepper. Add broth, stirring until mixed. Bring to a boil. Boil 1 minute, stirring constantly; reduce heat. Stir in peas. Cook 5 minutes, stirring constantly. Add chicken; mix well. Spoon into a greased 9x13-inch baking dish. Combine baking mix and remaining 2 teaspoons basil in a bowl; mix well. Add milk gradually, stirring constantly until moistened. Drop dough by tablespoonfuls over chicken mixture (about 12 dumplings). Bake at 350° for 30 minutes; cover. Bake 10 minutes longer or until dumplings are done. Yields 6–8 servings.

Hester P. Thompson, Birmingham Life Club (Book 4)

Basil-Lemon Turkey Breast

½ boneless turkey breast
½ cup chopped fresh basil
2 garlic cloves, minced
1 tablespoon grated lemon zest
2 lemons, thinly sliced
1½ cups thinly sliced carrots

¾ cup thinly sliced celery
1 Vidalia onion, chopped
1 cup water
1 cup reduced-sodium chicken
   broth
Steamed wild rice

Loosen the skin carefully on turkey breast. Combine basil, garlic, and lemon zest in a bowl and mix well. Spread basil mixture under the skin and arrange lemon slices over basil mixture. Combine carrots, celery, onion, and water in a roasting pan; mix well. Arrange a roasting rack over vegetable mixture. Place turkey on roasting rack. Roast at 325° for 1 hour or until meat thermometer placed in the thickest portion of turkey registers 170°, basting frequently. Remove turkey to a cutting board. Let stand for 20 minutes. Discard skin and slice.

Drain vegetable mixture. Combine vegetable mixture and broth in blender. Process until puréed. Pour into a saucepan. Cook until just heated through, stirring constantly. Serve warm with turkey and steamed wild rice. Yields 6 servings.

Gussie Evans, Mobile Council (Book 4)

Lemon Butter Cornish Hens

4 Cornish game hens
1 cup vodka
8 thin slices lemon
8 thin slices butter
2 teaspoons salt
1 teaspoon white pepper
2 teaspoons crushed tarragon

1½ sticks butter, softened
2 teaspoons finely grated lemon
  rind
3 tablespoons lemon juice
1½ cups chicken broth
2 tablespoons whipping cream
½ cup sour cream

Coat hens with vodka inside and out; let rest 15 minutes. Carefully loosen skin over breast with fingers, making a pocket. Place 2 slices lemon and 2 slices butter in the skin pockets of each hen. Season inside and out with a mixture of salt, white pepper, and tarragon. Place hens in a baking pan; coat with mixture of butter, lemon rind, and lemon juice. Pour chicken broth in bottom of baking pan. Bake at 450° for 15 minutes; baste. Reduce heat to 375°; cook for 30–45 minutes or until done. Remove Cornish hens from pan. Reduce pan liquids to ½ volume; add whipping cream and sour cream. Simmer to thicken.

Freida Burroughs, Riverchase Council (Book 2)

Seafood

1959
Princess

The desk set received a smart, new look. Compactness, attractive styling and illuminated dial (it lights up when you lift the handset or you can keep it on as a night light) contributed to the all-around usefulness of the Princess set. Featured in a variety or colors, including pastels, its design appealed to women and teenage girls. The Princess was unique in two aspects: it required an external electric transformer to power the light-up dial, and when production began it did not contain enough room for a bell ringer, so an external ringer was required. The Princess model remained in production until 1994 with several modifications throughout the years.

With the first transcontinental microwave transmitting system now in operation, true number calling is instituted—that is, seven numerical digits without letters or names—although it took more than fifteen years to implement throughout the system. But cables provide much higher signal quality, avoid atmospheric interference, and offer greater capacity and security.

Becky's Famous Shrimp Creole

¼ cup all-purpose flour
¼ cup bacon grease
1½ cups chopped onions
1 cup chopped green onions
1 cup chopped celery with
  leaves
1 cup chopped green bell
  pepper
2 cloves garlic, minced
1 (6-ounce) can tomato paste
1 (14½-ounce) can diced
  tomatoes, undrained

1 (8-ounce) can tomato sauce
1 cup water
5 teaspoons salt
1 teaspoon pepper
1 teaspoon Tabasco
2 or 3 bay leaves
1 teaspoon sugar
1 teaspoon Worcestershire
  sauce
1 tablespoon lemon juice
4 pounds shrimp, peeled,
  deveined

In a large roaster, make dark roux of flour and grease. Add onions, green onions, celery, bell pepper, and garlic; sauté till soft. Add tomato paste, tomatoes, tomato sauce, water, salt, pepper, Tabasco, bay leaves, sugar, Worcestershire, and lemon juice. Simmer 1 hour covered. Add shrimp and cook 15 minutes more. Serve over rice.

Becky Chastang, Mobile Council (Book 1)

Shrimp Creole

1 cup thinly sliced onions
1 cup thinly sliced celery
1 cup green bell pepper, cut into
  2-inch strips
¼ cup vegetable oil
3½ cups canned tomatoes
1 (8-ounce) can tomato sauce
2 bay leaves

1 tablespoon sugar
1 tablespoon salt
1 tablespoon chili powder
⅛ teaspoon Tabasco
2 pounds fresh shrimp, peeled,
  deveined
2 tablespoons flour
⅓ cup water

Sauté onions, celery, and bell pepper in oil in an electric skillet at 300° until tender. Add tomatoes, tomato sauce, bay leaves, sugar, salt, chili powder, and Tabasco sauce; mix well. Add shrimp. Cover and reduce heat. Simmer 30 minutes. Add flour and water and cook 5 minutes longer or until thickened. Remove bay leaves. Serve over rice. Yields 6 servings.

Eloise Bennett, Decatur Council (Book 4)

Garlic-Broiled Shrimp

2 pounds large shrimp
½ cup butter or margarine,
  melted
½ cup olive oil
¼ cup minced fresh parsley

1 tablespoon minced green
  onion
3 cloves garlic, minced
1½ tablespoons lemon juice
Coarsely ground black pepper

Peel shrimp, leaving tails on; devein and butterfly. Set shrimp aside. Combine next 6 ingredients in a large shallow dish. Add shrimp, tossing well to coat. Cover and marinate for at least 30 minutes. Broil shrimp 4 inches from heat for 3–4 minutes; turn and broil for an additional 3–4 minutes or until done. Sprinkle with pepper; serve with pan drippings.

Narice Sutton, Riverchase Council (Book 2)

Barbecue Shrimp

½ cup olive oil
3 sticks margarine, melted
4 drops Tabasco
1 lemon, sliced
1 cup white wine
2 garlic buds, minced

¼ teaspoon salt
¼ teaspoon pepper
¼ teaspoon oregano
1 tablespoon chili sauce
2 pounds shrimp (in shells)
Paprika

Mix all ingredients except shrimp and paprika. Marinate shrimp in mixture 1–2 hours. Bake at 350° for 30 minutes for large shrimp or 20 minutes for small shrimp, basting often. Sprinkle liberally with paprika.

Patsy Higginbottom, Birmingham Central Council (Book 2)

Shrimp Scampi

1 pound fresh shrimp, peeled,
    deveined, butterflied
½ stick butter
¼ cup dry white wine
¼ cup chopped green onions

1 garlic clove, minced
1 tablespoon chopped parsley
1 teaspoon salt
¼ teaspoon pepper

Combine shrimp, butter, wine, green onions, garlic, parsley, salt, and pepper in a large skillet. Cook 10–15 minutes or until shrimp turn pink and are cooked through. Yields 4 servings.

Betty Holloway, Birmingham Life Club (Book 4)

Low-Fat Shrimp Étouffée

2 tablespoons flour
¼ cup butter, melted
¼ cup finely chopped celery
2 tablespoons finely chopped
  green onions
1 clove garlic, minced
1 cup water

2 tablespoons chopped parsley
1½ pounds fresh or frozen
  peeled shrimp
1 teaspoon salt
Cayenne pepper to taste
3 cups hot cooked rice

Cook flour in butter in 3-quart saucepan 5 minutes or until golden brown, stirring frequently. Stir in celery, green onions, and garlic. Cook 3–4 minutes, stirring constantly. Stir in water, parsley, shrimp, salt, and cayenne pepper. Simmer, covered, 15 minutes. Serve over rice. Yields 6 servings.

Hildegarde Killoch, Bon Secour Life Club (Book 3)

In the early days, operators working at a large switchboard would answer an incoming telephone call and connect it manually to the party being called. The first automatic telephone exchange was patented by Almon Strowger of Kansas City in 1891 and installed in 1892, but manual switchboards remained in common use. The last manual switchboard in the Southern Bell region was removed from service in Rosedale, Mississippi, on September 21, 1969.

Crunchy Shrimp Casserole

3 cups cooked shrimp
1 cup diced onions
1 cup diced pimentos
2 cups diced celery
10 ounces sharp cheese, cubed

1 (8-ounce) can sliced water
  chestnuts
1 cup sliced almonds
2 cups Hellmann's mayonnaise
Ritz Cracker crumbs for topping

Combine all ingredients, except Ritz Cracker crumbs; mix well. Pour into large glass baking dish; top with crumbs. Bake at 350° for 30–45 minutes. Makes 10 servings.

Note: May substitute chicken or ham for shrimp.

Jean Ivey, Riverchase Council (Book 1)

Victoria Crab Cakes

2 eggs, beaten
½ cup chopped onion
½ cup each: chopped green
  and red bell pepper
3 tablespoons white
  Worcestershire
1 tablespoon lemon juice

1 teaspoon dry mustard
½–1 teaspoon ground red
  pepper
1 pound fresh lump crabmeat
2 cups seasoned Italian bread
  crumbs, divided
2–4 tablespoons butter

Combine eggs, onion, bell peppers, Worcestershire, lemon juice, dry mustard, and red pepper in bowl; mix well. Stir in crabmeat and 1 cup bread crumbs; mix well. Shape into 8 patties. Coat with remaining 1 cup bread crumbs. Brown on both sides in butter in skillet over medium heat; drain. Yields 8 servings.

Donna Nix, Huntsville Council (Book 3)

Crabmeat Casserole

7 pieces bread, crust removed, cut into ½-inch strips
1 pound crabmeat (or 4 cans), drained
½ cup diced onion
½ cup diced bell pepper
½ cup diced celery

1½ cups grated sharp Cheddar cheese, divided
4 eggs
1 cup milk, divided
1 (10¾-ounce) can cream of mushroom soup

Line casserole with ½ the bread strips. In bowl, mix crabmeat, onion, bell pepper, celery, and ½ cup cheese. Spoon over bread; add rest of bread to form another layer. Mix eggs with ½ cup milk; pour over mixture. Mix soup with remaining ½ cup milk and pour over. Top with remaining 1 cup cheese. Bake 45–60 minutes at 350°. Serves 10.

Candy Byrd, Birmingham South Council (Book 1)

Oven-Fried Fish

1 pound fish fillets
½ cup milk
½ cup fine bread crumbs

Salt and pepper to taste
¼ stick butter, melted

Dip fillets in milk and coat with bread crumbs. Place on a well-greased baking sheet. Season with salt and pepper. Drizzle with melted butter. Bake at 400° until fish flakes easily and is golden brown. Yields 4 servings.

Sue Small, Selma Life Club (Book 4)

Crunchy Fried Fish

2 pounds fish fillets	1 cup lukewarm water
Salt and pepper to taste	1 tablespoon oil
1 cup all-purpose flour	1 egg white, stiffly beaten
1 egg yolk	Oil for frying

Dry fish; sprinkle with salt and pepper. In shallow bowl, put flour and drop egg yolk in center. Add water and 1 tablespoon oil; stir well. Fold egg white into batter. Dip fillets in batter and fry until golden brown on both sides.

Curtis N. Jackson, Gadsden Counccil (Book 2)

Baked Fish

2 tablespoons instant minced onion	2 tablespoons canola oil
	1/8 teaspoon garlic powder
2 tablespoons water	1 1/2 tablespoons lemon juice
1/2 tablespoon basil	1 pound white fish fillets
1/2 teaspoon paprika	1 teaspoon parsley

Combine minced onion and water in a small bowl and let stand 10 minutes. Add basil, paprika, canola oil, garlic powder, and lemon juice; mix well. Pour herb mixture over fillets in a greased 6x10-inch baking pan. Bake at 350° for 10–15 minutes or until fish flakes easily. Sprinkle with parsley and serve immediately. You may use cod, halibut, or any white fish in this recipe. Yields 4 servings.

Gussie Evans, Mobile Council (Book 4)

Lemon-Battered Fish

1½ cups all-purpose flour, divided
⅔ cup water
⅔ cup lemon juice, divided
1 egg, beaten

1 teaspoon baking powder
½ teaspoon sugar
¾ teaspoon salt
1 pound fresh or frozen fish fillets

Combine 1 cup flour, water, ⅓ cup lemon juice, egg, baking powder, sugar, and salt in bowl; mix well. Dip fish in remaining ⅓ cup lemon juice; coat with remaining ½ cup flour. Dip into batter, coating well. Deep-fry in hot oil until golden brown. Yields 3 servings.

Dorothy Kimbrough, Decatur Council (Book 3)

Baked Bass

2 pounds bass fillets
2 tablespoons butter, melted
1 lime, thinly sliced

1 lemon, thinly sliced
1 small orange, thinly sliced
1 bell pepper, finely chopped

Place fillets skin side down in a greased baking dish; brush with butter. Arrange fruit slices over fillets in alternating pattern and sprinkle on bell pepper. Bake at 350° for 30 minutes or until fish flakes with a fork easily. Serves 4.

George Ponder, Decatur Council (Book 1)

Grilled Sweet and Sour Bluefish

1 cup water
1 onion, minced
1 red pepper, minced
½ stick unsalted butter
¼ cup white wine vinegar
1 tablespoon dark brown sugar
1 tablespoon Worcestershire

2 teaspoons pepper, or to taste
2 teaspoons sweet paprika
2 teaspoons chili powder
1 teaspoon minced garlic
1 teaspoon salt
6 (½-pound) bluefish fillets

In a stainless steel or enameled saucepan, combine water, onion, red pepper, butter, vinegar, sugar, Worcestershire, pepper, paprika, chili powder, garlic, and salt; bring liquid to a boil, then simmer for 15 minutes. Keep sauce warm.

Grill fillets skin side down over glowing coals about 4 inches from heat, basting with sauce, for 6–8 minutes or until they just flake when tested with a fork. Transfer fillets with a large spatula to heated plates and serve remaining sauce in a heated sauceboat. Serves 6.

Katherine Creamer, Mobile Council (Book 1)

Salmon Croquettes

1 (15-ounce) can pink salmon, drained, deboned, flaked
1 cup evaporated milk, divided
1½ cups crushed cornflakes, divided
¼ cup dill pickle relish
¼ cup finely chopped celery
2 tablespoons finely chopped onion
Vegetable oil for deep-frying

Combine salmon, ½ cup evaporated milk, ½ cup crushed corn-flakes, pickle relish, celery, and onion in a large bowl; mix well. Shape by ¼ cupfuls into oval shapes. Dip in remaining ½ cup evaporated milk and coat with remaining 1 cup crushed corn-flakes.

Heat oil in a deep fryer to 365°. Deep-fry croquettes a few at a time for 2½ minutes or until golden brown. Remove to paper towels to drain. Keep warm until serving time. Serve croquettes with Tartar Sauce. Yields 4–6 servings.

TARTAR SAUCE:
⅔ cup evaporated milk
¼ cup mayonnaise
2 tablespoons dill pickle relish
1 tablespoon finely chopped onion

Combine evaporated milk, mayonnaise, pickle relish, and onion in medium saucepan. Cook over medium-low heat until slightly thickened and heated through. Serve warm. Yields 1 cup.

Hester P. Thompson, Birmingham Life Club (Book 4)

Easy Salmon Cakes

1 (12-ounce) can pink salmon,
  skin removed
⅓ cup chopped onion
1 egg, lightly beaten

½ cup flour
1½ teaspoons baking powder
1½ cups vegetable oil

Drain salmon, reserving 2 tablespoons juice. Combine salmon, reserved juice, onion, egg, flour, and baking powder in a large bowl; mix well. Shape into 6 balls and flatten into patties. Heat oil in a large skillet. Cook salmon patties in oil on each side until golden brown. Remove to paper towels to drain. Yields 4–6 servings.

Jane B. Weatherly, Mobile Council (Book 4)

Cakes

1964
Touch-Tone

As America neared the 200 million mark in population, a new era in telephoning services began with push-button calling. Touch-Tone service was introduced, limiting errors and increasing the speed of dialing. A keypad replaced the familiar rotary "pulse" dial, and early Touch-Tone sets had only ten buttons. (The * and # keys were added in 1968.) The Touch-Tone system could travel across microwave transmitter links and work rapidly with solid state computer-controlled phone exchanges. A tone is produced as long as a key is depressed. No matter how long you press, the tone is decoded as the appropriate digit. The shortest duration in which a digit can be sent and decoded is about 100 milliseconds by automatic dialers. A twelve-digit long-distance phone number can be dialed by an automatic phone dialer in a little more than a second—about as long as it takes a pulse dial to send a single "0" digit.

Chocolate Pound Cake

3 cups cake flour
½ cup cocoa
1 teaspoon baking powder
¼ teaspoon salt
2 sticks margarine, softened

½ cup Crisco
3 cups sugar
5 whole eggs
1¼ cups sweet milk
1 teaspoon vanilla

Mix dry ingredients. Cream margarine, Crisco, and sugar; add eggs one at a time, beating after each. Add milk, vanilla, and dry ingredients. Pour into greased and floured Bundt pan. Cook at 300° for 1½–2 hours. Do not open oven door until 1½ hours is up.

CHOCOLATE ICING (OPTIONAL):
⅔ cup evaporated milk
2 cups sugar
¼ cup cocoa

¼ teaspoon salt
1 stick margarine
1 teaspoon vanilla

In saucepan, mix milk, sugar, cocoa, and salt; boil for 2 minutes. Take off heat and add margarine and vanilla. Beat with mixer until creamy.

Dilla Samuel, Anniston Council (Book 1)

Crusty Pound Cake

1½ cups butter, softened
3 cups sugar
6 eggs
1 tablespoon vanilla extract

1 teaspoon almond extract
3 cups all-purpose flour
½ teaspoon salt

Cream butter well in a large mixing bowl. Add sugar gradually, mixing until texture is fine and mealy. Add eggs, one at a time, beating after each addition. Add flavorings. Combine flour and salt; stir flour mixture into batter, beating until flour is moistened. Do not overbeat. Pour into a greased and floured 10-inch tube pan. Bake at 325° for 1 hour and 25 minutes, or until a toothpick inserted comes out clean and cake shrinks from sides of pan. Cool in pan 15 minutes. Turn out onto a wire rack; turn right side up and complete cooling.

Willie Mae Crews, Birmingham East Council (Book 1)

Sour Cream Pound Cake

3 cups all-purpose flour
¼ teaspoon baking soda
3 cups sugar
2 sticks margarine, softened

1 (8-ounce) carton sour cream
1½ teaspoons almond extract
6 eggs

Measure out flour in a bowl and add soda to it. In separate bowl, cream sugar and margarine well; add sour cream and almond extract; mix well. Add eggs, one at a time, and mix well after each. Add flour mixture, ½ at a time, and mix well after each addition. Pour into a well-greased and floured tube pan and bake at 325° for 1½ hours. Do not bake over 1½ hours. Cool for 10 minutes in pan before turning out.

Mary Ann McDowell, Riverchase Council (Book 2)

Prize-Winning Pound Cake

2 sticks butter, softened
½ cup Crisco
3 cups sugar
6 eggs
3½ cups sifted all-purpose
  flour
½ teaspoon baking powder
⅛ teaspoon salt
1 cup milk
2 teaspoons vanilla*

Preheat oven to 300°. Cream butter, shortening, and sugar. Add eggs, one at a time; alternately add dry ingredients and milk. Add flavoring; mix well. Pour into greased and floured tube pan; bake 1½ hours at 300°. Cool 15 minutes on rack, then turn onto plate.

Note: *May substitute 1 teaspoon lemon flavoring, 1 teaspoon orange flavoring, 1 teaspoon vanilla flavoring, or 2 teaspoons rum for the 2 teaspoons vanilla.

Betty Yancey, Birmingham Central Council (Book 2)

Cream Cheese Pound Cake

1½ cups margarine, softened
1 (8-ounce) package cream
  cheese, softened
3 cups sugar
Salt to taste
1 teaspoon vanilla extract
1 teaspoon almond extract
3 cups all-purpose flour
6 eggs, room temperature

Cream margarine, cream cheese, and sugar in mixer bowl until light and fluffy. Add salt and flavorings; mix well. Add flour alternately with eggs, mixing well after each addition. Spoon into greased and floured tube pan. Bake at 300° for 1½ hours. Cool in pan on wire rack; remove to serving plate. Yields 16 servings.

Mattie Foster, Huntsville Life Club (Book 3)

Seven-Up Pound Cake

1½ cups butter, softened
3 cups sugar
5 eggs

3 cups sifted all-purpose flour
2 tablespoons lemon extract
¾ cup 7-Up

Cream butter and sugar until fluffy; add eggs, one at a time. Combine well. Add flour. Beat in lemon extract and 7-Up. Pour mixture into well-greased Bundt or tube pan; bake 1–1¼ hours at 325°.

Peggy Hawkins (Book 1)

Butter Peach Pound Cake

3 cups self-rising flour
2¼ cups sugar
3 sticks margarine, melted
¾ cup milk

6 eggs
1 teaspoon lemon extract
1 teaspoon vanilla extract
1 cup mashed fresh peaches

Combine flour, sugar, margarine, milk, eggs, lemon extract, and vanilla in a mixing bowl. Beat at medium speed for 20 minutes. Fold in peaches. Pour into a greased and floured tube pan. Place on rack in a cold oven. Bake at 300° for 70 minutes or until cake tests done. Cool on wire rack. Yields 16 servings.

Mary Alice Neal, Birmingham Life Club (Book 4)

Butter Pecan Bundt Cake

Sugar
Chopped pecans
1 (18¼-ounce) package butter
  pecan cake mix
1 cup water

1 cup vegetable oil
4 eggs
1 (16-ounce) can coconut pecan
  icing

Grease a big Bundt pan with nonstick cooking spray. Sprinkle with sugar and pecans. Combine cake mix, water, oil, eggs, and icing in a mixing bowl and beat well. Pour into prepared pan. Bake at 350° for 50 minutes or until cake tests done. Cool in pan for 10 minutes. Invert onto a wire rack to cool completely. Yields 16 servings.

Paula D. Smith, Birmingham Metro Council (Book 4)

The dial telephone was invented by Almon Strowger of St. Louis, Missouri, who patented the automatic telephone exchange in 1891. Mr. Strowger, a mortician, developed the method of direct dialing because he felt exchange operators were diverting his business calls to his competitors. The dial phone was not put into service until 1905 when Dial Switching Equipment was developed. Now, all of this switching equipment has been replaced by computer circuitry.

Sock-It-To-Me Cake

1 (18¼-ounce) package butter
  recipe cake mix
1 cup sour cream
½ cup vegetable oil
¼ cup sugar
¼ cup water
4 eggs

Combine cake mix, sour cream, oil, sugar, water, and eggs in a mixing bowl and beat until moistened. Beat at high speed for 2 minutes. Pour ⅔ of batter into a greased and floured Bundt pan. Sprinkle with Filling. Spread remaining batter over Filling. Bake at 375° for 45–55 minutes or until cake springs back when lightly touched. Cool in pan 25 minutes. Invert onto a serving plate. Drizzle Glaze over cake. Yields 16 servings.

FILLING:
1 cup chopped pecans
2 tablespoons brown sugar
2 teaspoons cinnamon

Combine pecans, brown sugar, and cinnamon in a bowl; mix well. Yields about 1 cup.

GLAZE:
1 cup confectioners' sugar
2 tablespoons milk

Combine confectioners' sugar and milk in a bowl; mix until smooth. Yields 1 cup.

Mary Gillis, Mobile Council (Book 4)

Red Velvet Cake

This makes a large gorgeous red cake with icing that never hardens. Sure to be a conversation piece.

2½ cups sifted cake flour
½ teaspoon salt
3 tablespoons instant chocolate mix
½ cup butter, softened
1½ cups sugar
2 eggs

2 (1-ounce) bottles red food coloring
1 teaspoon vanilla
1 cup buttermilk
1 tablespoon white vinegar
1 teaspoon baking soda

Sift together flour, salt, and instant chocolate mix. Cream butter and sugar. When well creamed, beat in whole eggs, one at a time. Blend well and add food coloring and vanilla. Mix buttermilk, vinegar, and soda; add alternately with dry ingredients to creamed mixture. Blend at low speed on electric mixer between each addition. Grease and line 2 (9-inch) cake pans. (They must be 1½ inches deep, as cake rises high.) Pour in batter and bake in preheated 350° oven about 30 minutes or until done; don't overbake. Remove from oven and cool on racks 15 minutes. Remove from pans and continue cooling on racks before frosting. Frost with Mystery Icing.

MYSTERY ICING:

4 tablespoons all-purpose flour
1 cup sweet milk
1 cup granulated sugar

1 stick margarine, softened
½ cup shortening
3 teaspoons vanilla
¼ teaspoon salt

Blend flour and milk. Cook until mixture thickens to consistency of cream; cool, but don't chill. Cream sugar, margarine, and shortening, adding vanilla and salt. Add slightly cooked flour mixture and continue beating until fluffy. Spread generously between layers and over all the cake.

Jewel Edney, Riverchase Council (Book 1)

White Chocolate Cake

4 ounces white chocolate
½ cup boiling water
1 cup butter or margarine,
  softened
2 cups sugar
4 egg yolks, unbeaten

1 teaspoon vanilla
2½ cups sifted cake flour
½ teaspoon salt
1 teaspoon baking soda
1 cup buttermilk
4 egg whites, stiffly beaten

Melt chocolate in boiling water; cool. Cream butter and sugar until fluffy. Add egg yolks, one at a time, and beat well after each. Add melted chocolate mixture and vanilla; mix well. Sift together flour, salt, and soda; add alternately with buttermilk to chocolate mixture; beat until smooth. Fold in whites. Pour in 3 deep 8- or 9-inch layer pans, lined on bottoms with parchment paper. Bake in moderate 350° oven for 30–40 minutes; cool. Frost top and sides.

RICH WHITE CHOCOLATE FROSTING:

4 ounces white chocolate
¾ cup confectioners' sugar
Dash of salt
2 tablespoons hot water

1 egg yolk
2 tablespoons butter
½ teaspoon vanilla

Melt chocolate; blend in sugar, salt, and hot water. Add yolk; beat well. Add butter, 1 tablespoon at a time, beating thoroughly after each. Stir in vanilla.

Rosemary Parker, Birmingham Central Council (Book 1)

Tunnel of Fudge Cake

1½ cups butter, softened
6 eggs
1½ cups sugar
4⅓ cups chocolate frosting
  mix, divided

2 cups all-purpose flour
2 cups chopped pecans
2½ cups water

Cream butter in large mixer bowl until light and fluffy. Add eggs, 1 at a time, beating 1 minute or longer after each addition. Add sugar gradually, beating constantly until smooth. Stir in 3⅓ cups frosting mix, flour, and pecans. Spoon into greased and floured 12-cup Bundt pan. Bake at 350° for 60–65 minutes or until cake pulls from side of pan. Cool in pan for up to 1 hour; center will be softer if removed earlier. Invert onto serving plate. Combine remaining 1 cup frosting mix with water in small bowl; mix well. Spoon over cake. Store in airtight container. May serve warm with ice cream and chocolate syrup. Yields 16 servings.

Vickie Capuzzo, Birmingham South Council (Book 3)

The mobile telephone was invented by Bell Telephone Company and introduced into New York City police cars in 1924. Although the first commercial mobile telephone service became available in St. Louis, Missouri, in 1946, the mobile telephone would not become common for another four decades.

Better Than Sex

1 (18¼-ounce) box yellow
butter cake mix
1 (8-ounce) package sweet
chocolate chips
1 (8-ounce) package chopped
pecans
1 (3-ounce) box French vanilla
instant pudding mix

½ box unsweetened German's
chocolate, grated
1 (8-ounce) carton sour cream
½ cup Wesson oil
½ cup sweet milk
4 eggs
1 stick butter or margarine

Mix all ingredients well. Pour into a greased and floured tube or Bundt pan; bake 1 hour at 350° or until done.

ICING:

1 (8-ounce) package cream
cheese, softened
1 (1-pound) box confectioners'
sugar

1 teaspoon vanilla
Chopped nuts or coconut
(optional)

Cream cheese and sugar until smooth; add vanilla, nuts, and coconut. Spread on cooled cake.

Mary C. Martin, Birmingham East Council (Book 1)

Volcano Cake

1 (3-ounce) can flaked coconut
2 cups chopped pecans
1 (18¼-ounce) package
  German chocolate cake mix
½ cup margarine

1 (8-ounce) package cream
  cheese
1 (1-pound) package
  confectioners' sugar

Mix coconut and pecans in bowl. Spread in greased 9x13-inch cake pan. Prepare cake mix using package directions. Spread in prepared cake pan. Combine margarine and cream cheese in saucepan. Heat until softened. Add confectioners' sugar; mix well. Drop by spoonfuls over cake batter. Tap bottom of pan on counter, but do not stir. Bake at 350° for 45 minutes. Cool on wire rack. Serve with vanilla ice cream. Yields 15 servings.

Nancy Morgan, Decatur Council (Book 3)

Butterfinger Cake

1 (18¼-ounce) package yellow
  cake mix
1 (8-ounce) jar caramel ice
  cream topping
1 (14-ounce) can sweetened
  condensed milk

2 large Butterfinger candy bars,
  crushed
1 (16-ounce) carton whipped
  topping

Prepare and bake cake mix using package directions for 9x13-inch cake pan. Pierce cake several times with handle of wooden spoon. Mix topping and condensed milk in bowl. Pour over cake. Sprinkle with half the candy crumbs. Spread with whipped topping. Sprinkle with remaining crumbs. Chill until serving time. Yields 15 servings.

Dot Johnson, Anniston Council (Book 3)

Milky Way Cake

8 mini Milky Way candy
  bars
½ cup butter or margarine,
  melted
1½ cups sugar
½ cup butter or margarine,
  softened

4 eggs, separated
1 teaspoon vanilla extract
1¼ cups buttermilk
½ teaspoon baking soda
3 cups all-purpose flour
1 cup chopped pecans

Combine candy bars and melted butter in saucepan; place over low heat until candy bars are melted, stirring constantly. Cool. Cream sugar and softened butter until light and fluffy; add egg yolks, one at a time, beating well after each addition; stir in vanilla.

Combine buttermilk and soda; add to creamed mixture alternately with flour, beating well after each addition. Stir in candy bar mixture and pecans. Fold in stiffly beaten egg whites. Pour batter into a greased and floured 10-inch tube pan; bake at 325° for 1 hour and 35 minutes or until well done. Let cool in pan 1 hour; remove from pan, and complete cooling on wire rack. Frost with milk chocolate frosting, if desired. Yields 1 (10-inch) cake.

Opal Mofitt, Tuscaloosa Pioneer Unit (Book 1)

Cakes

Fudge Cake

2 sticks butter, softened
2 cups sugar
2 eggs
2 teaspoons vanilla extract

2 cups all-purpose flour
1¼ cups milk
½ cup baking cocoa
½ teaspoon baking powder

Cream butter and sugar in a mixing bowl until light and fluffy. Add eggs and vanilla; beat well. Add flour, milk, baking cocoa, and baking powder; mix well. The batter will be thin. Pour into a greased 9x13-inch cake pan. Bake at 350° for 30 minutes or until cake tests done. Cool on wire rack. Yields 15 servings.

Susan Ragland, Birmingham South Cahaba Council (Book 4)

Peanut Butter Cake

CAKE:
2 cups sugar
1¾ cups self-rising flour
3 eggs
1 cup milk
1 cup vegetable oil, or 2 sticks
  margarine, melted

1 cup peanut butter
1 teaspoon vanilla extract
Frosting

Mix sugar and flour in a mixing bowl. Add eggs, milk, oil, peanut butter, and vanilla; beat well. Pour into 3 greased and floured cake pans. Bake at 350° for 45 minutes or until layers test done. Spread the hot Frosting over layers. Yields 12 servings.

FROSTING:
1 cup peanut butter
½ stick margarine

¼ cup milk
2 cups confectioners' sugar

Combine peanut butter, margarine, milk, and confectioners' sugar in a saucepan. Cook over medium heat until smooth. Yields 3 cups.

Fay Clark, Riverchase Council (Book 4)

Mississippi Mud Sheet Cake

2 cups sugar
⅓ cup baking cocoa
1 cup vegetable oil
4 eggs
½ cup milk
1½ cups all-purpose flour

1 tablespoon vanilla extract
¼ teaspoon salt
1 cup chopped pecans
1 (10-ounce) package miniature
  marshmallows

Combine sugar, cocoa, oil, eggs, milk, flour, vanilla, and salt in mixer bowl; beat until smooth. Stir in pecans. Spoon into greased and floured 10x14-inch cake pan. Bake at 300° for 40–50 minutes or until cake tests done. Sprinkle with marshmallows.

FROSTING:

½ cup butter, melted
⅓ cup baking cocoa
1 (1-pound) package
  confectioners' sugar

⅓ cup milk
1 teaspoon vanilla extract
½ cup chopped pecans

Combine butter, cocoa, sugar, milk, and vanilla in mixer bowl; mix well. Stir in pecans. Spread over marshmallows on cake. Yields 24 servings.

Flo Thompson, Birmingham South Cahaba Council (Book 3)

Authentic Black Forest Cake

Not a "quickie"—this is the real thing! This is not just a cake, it's a showpiece!

CAKE:

2 eggs, separated	⅓ cup oil
1½ cups sugar, divided	1 cup milk, divided
1¾ cups sifted cake flour	2 ounces unsweetened
¾ teaspoon baking soda	chocolate, melted, cooled
1 teaspoon salt	

Beat egg whites until soft peaks form. Gradually add ½ cup sugar, beating until stiff peaks form. Sift together flour, remaining 1 cup sugar, soda, and salt into mixing bowl. Add oil and ½ cup milk. Beat for 1 minute at medium speed on mixer, scraping bowl often. Add remaining ½ cup milk, egg yolks, and chocolate. Beat 1 minute longer, scraping bowl frequently. Gently fold in egg whites.

Pour into 2 greased and floured 9-inch round pans. Bake at 350° for 30–35 minutes. Cool 10 minutes; remove from pans. Cool thoroughly. Split each layer in half to make 4 thin layers; set aside.

CHERRY FILLING:

1 (20-ounce) can pitted tart	1 tablespoon Kirsch
red cherries, drained	3 drops almond extract
½ cup port wine	

Combine all ingredients. Chill 3–4 hours or overnight; drain thoroughly.

CHOCOLATE MOUSSE:

3 ounces semisweet chocolate	1 cup whipping cream
3 tablespoons Kirsch	2 tablespoons sugar
1 egg, well beaten	

Combine chocolate and Kirsch in top of double boiler; stir over—not touching—boiling water until smoothly melted. Slowly stir into egg. Whip cream with sugar; fold into cooled chocolate. Chill 2 hours.

(continued)

(Authentic Black Forest Cake continued)

Prepare Butter Frosting and chill 30 minutes before assembling.

BUTTER FROSTING:

6 tablespoons sweet butter   ⅓ cup light cream, divided
1 (1-pound) package sifted   1½ teaspoons vanilla
  confectioners' sugar, divided

Cream butter. Gradually add ½ the sugar, blending well. Beat in 2 tablespoons of the cream and all the vanilla. Gradually blend in remaining sugar. Add enough cream to make of spreading consistency.

Assembly: Spread ½ cup of frosting on the cut side of a cake layer. With remaining frosting, make 1 ridge ½ inch wide and ¾ inch high around outside edge of same cake layer; make another ridge 2 inches from outside edge. Chill for 30 minutes. Fill spaces with Cherry Filling. Spread second cake layer with Chocolate Mousse and place unfrosted side atop first. Chill for 30 minutes.

WHIPPED CREAM TOPPING:

2 cups whipping cream   1 teaspoon vanilla
2 tablespoons sugar

Whip cream with sugar and vanilla. Spread third cake layer with 1½ cups whipped cream and place atop second layer. Top with fourth cake layer. Reserving ¼ cup whipped cream, frost sides with remainder. Sift confectioners' sugar over top. Garnish with dollops of whipped cream, maraschino cherries, and chocolate curls. Chill for 2 hours before serving.

Brandon Kincaid, Birmingham Central Council (Book 2)

Aunt Pauline's Poor Man's Cake

½ (15-ounce) package raisins
1 cup sugar
½ cup shortening
Pinch of salt
½ teaspoon nutmeg
½ teaspoon ground cloves

½ teaspoon cinnamon
½ teaspoon allspice
½ cup chopped pecans
2 cups all-purpose flour
2 teaspoons baking powder

Combine raisins with water to cover in a saucepan. Bring to a boil. Boil 10 minutes. Stir in sugar and shortening. Let stand until cool. Add salt, nutmeg, cloves, cinnamon, allspice, and pecans; mix well. Stir in flour and baking powder. Pour into a greased and floured 9x13-inch cake pan. Bake at 300° for 25 minutes or until cake tests done. Cool on wire rack. Yields 15 servings.

Marion Thompson, Gadsden Life Club (Book 4)

Hillbilly Cake

1½ cups sugar
2 eggs
½ cup margarine, melted
2 cups all-purpose flour
2 teaspoons baking soda

1 (20-ounce) can crushed
   pineapple, undrained
1 cup packed brown sugar
1 cup chopped walnuts

Combine sugar, eggs, and margarine in mixer bowl; beat until smooth. Add flour, baking soda, and pineapple; mix well. Spoon into greased 9x13-inch cake pan. Sprinkle with brown sugar and walnuts. Bake at 350° for 40 minutes. Yields 15 servings.

Imogene Davis, Birmingham Life Club (Book 3)

Plum Cake

2 cups self-rising flour
2 cups sugar
2 jars strained plum baby food
3 eggs

1 teaspoon ground cloves
1 teaspoon cinnamon
1 cup vegetable oil
Chopped pecans

Mix all ingredients together with a spoon (do not use mixer). Bake in greased and floured Bundt pan 50 minutes at 350°.

Bonnie Hall, Mobile Council (Book 1)

Pistachio Cake

½ cup chopped nuts
½ cup chocolate chips
1 (3-ounce) package pistachio
  instant pudding
1 (18¼-ounce) package yellow
  cake mix

½ cup sugar
½ cup vegetable oil
1 cup water
4 eggs
1 (5-ounce) can chocolate syrup

Preheat oven to 350°. Grease and flour Bundt pan. Mix nuts and chocolate chips; sprinkle in bottom of pan. Combine remaining ingredients except chocolate syrup; mix 2 minutes or more. Take out 1 cup batter and mix in chocolate syrup. Pour remaining batter in pan. Then pour chocolate batter around top. Run knife through batter; bake 1 hour. Let sit in pan 10 minutes before taking out.

Rosemary Parker, Birmingham Central Council (Book 1)

Candi's Eggnog Cake

1 (18¼-ounce) package yellow
  cake mix
1 cup eggnog
¼ cup vegetable oil
3 eggs
3 tablespoons rum
¼ teaspoon nutmeg

1 (8-ounce) package cream
  cheese, softened
1 (1-pound) package
  confectioners' sugar
1½ teaspoons eggnog
Several drops of yellow food
  coloring

Combine first 6 ingredients in mixer bowl; beat at medium speed
3 minutes. Spoon into 3 greased and floured 8x8-inch cake pans.
Bake at 350° for 20 minutes or until cake tests done. Cool in pans
10 minutes; remove to wire rack to cool completely.

Beat cream cheese in mixer bowl until fluffy. Add confectioners'
sugar gradually, beating constantly until smooth. Beat in 1½ teaspoons eggnog ½ teaspoon at a time. Add food coloring; mix well.
Spread between layers and over top and side of cake. May substitute 1 teaspoon rum extract for rum. Yields 16 servings.

Mera Roberts, Mobile Life Club (Book 3)

Orange-Glazed Carrot Cake

2 teaspoons baking soda
⅓ cup buttermilk
1 teaspoon lemon extract
3 cups all-purpose flour
1 teaspoon baking powder
1 teaspoon cinnamon
½ teaspoon salt

1½ cups vegetable oil
2½ cups sugar, divided
4 eggs
3 cups grated carrots
½ cup orange juice
½ cup chopped pecans

Combine baking soda, buttermilk, and lemon extract in bowl; stir until baking soda is dissolved. Sift flour, baking powder, cinnamon, and salt together. Combine oil, 2 cups sugar, and eggs in mixer bowl. Beat until thick. Add buttermilk mixture, carrots, and flour mixture alternately to egg mixture, beating well by hand after each addition. Pour into greased and floured tube pan. Bake at 250° for 1½–2 hours or until cake tests done. Mix orange juice, remaining ½ cup sugar, and pecans in bowl. Spread over hot cake. Cool in pan. Yields 16 servings.

Jane Green, Riverchase Council (Book 3)

Carrot Cake

2 cups all-purpose flour
2 cups sugar
1 teaspoon salt
2 teaspoons baking soda

2 teaspoons cinnamon
1½ cups vegetable oil
4 eggs
3 cups grated carrots

Sift flour, sugar, salt, baking soda, and cinnamon into a mixing bowl. Add oil; mix well. Add eggs 1 at a time, beating well after each addition. Add carrots. Pour into a greased and floured 9x13-inch cake pan. Bake at 350° for 45 minutes. Cool on a wire rack. Spread Icing over cooled cake. Yields 15 servings.

ICING:

1 (8-ounce) package cream
   cheese, softened
1 stick butter, softened
1 teaspoon vanilla extract

1 (1-pound) package
   confectioners' sugar
Crushed nuts
Shredded coconut (optional)

Beat cream cheese, butter, and vanilla in mixing bowl until light and fluffy. Add confectioners' sugar and beat well. Stir in nuts and coconut. Yields 5–5½ cups.

Jo Anne Norris Emery, Bon Secour Life Club (Book 4)

Pineapple Yum-Yum Cake

1 (18¼-ounce) package yellow
   cake mix
3 eggs
1½ cups cold water
1 (3-ounce) package vanilla
   instant pudding mix
⅓ cup vegetable oil
1 (8-ounce) package cream
   cheese, softened

1 cup sour cream
¼ cup confectioners' sugar
1 (12-ounce) container
   whipped topping
1 (3-ounce) package French
   vanilla instant pudding mix
1 (20-ounce) can crushed
   pineapple, drained, reserve
   juice

Combine cake mix, eggs, water, vanilla pudding mix, and oil in a mixing bowl; mix well. Pour into 3 greased 9-inch cake pans. Bake at 350° for 20–25 minutes or until layers test done. Cool in pans for 5 minutes. Remove to a paper towel- or wax-paper-lined surface to cool completely.

Beat cream cheese and sour cream in a mixing bowl until smooth and creamy. Beat in confectioners' sugar, whipped topping, and French vanilla pudding mix. Fold in drained pineapple. Drizzle each layer with ⅓ of the reserved pineapple juice. Spread pineapple mixture between layers and over top and side of cake. Chill, covered, for 2 days before serving (to enhance the flavor). You may store in refrigerator 2 weeks. Yields 12 servings.

Mauntez Mayer, Anniston Council (Book 4)

Pecan Pie Cake

1 (18¼-ounce) package yellow
  cake mix

1 egg
½ cup butter, melted

Mix ingredients really well. Reserve ⅔ cup batter. Pour remainder into a greased 9x13-inch pan and bake at 325° for 15 minutes or until brown.

FILLING:

1½ cups white Karo syrup
⅔ cup reserved batter
½ cup dark brown sugar,
  packed

3 eggs
1 teaspoon vanilla
1–2 cups chopped pecans

Combine ingredients; pour on top of above crust. Bake about 1 hour at 325°.

Rosemary Parker, Birmingham Central Council (Book 1)

Apple Pie Cake

1 stick margarine
1 (18¼-ounce) box yellow
  cake mix
1 (20-ounce) can apple slices
  (not pie filling)

1 tablespoon cinnamon
½ cup sugar
1 (8-ounce) carton sour cream
1 egg

Mix margarine and cake mix until crumbly. Press into ungreased 9x13-inch pan, building sides up a little. Bake at 350° for 10 minutes. Pour apple slices over crust while still warm. Mix cinnamon and sugar together; sprinkle over apples. Mix sour cream and egg together; spoon on top of mixture. Bake at 350° for 25 minutes.

Rosemary Parker, Birmingham Central Council (Book 2)

Apple Dapple Cake

2 cups sugar
1¼ cups vegetable oil
4 eggs
2 cups self-rising flour

3 cups finely chopped apples
1 cup chopped pecans
1 teaspoon cinnamon
1 teaspoon vanilla extract

Cream sugar and oil in mixer bowl until light and fluffy. Add eggs, flour, apples, pecans, cinnamon, and vanilla. Beat until smooth. Pour into greased Bundt pan. Bake at 325° for 1–1¼ hours or until cake tests done. Yields 16 servings.

Lola Duffey, Shoals Life Club (Book 3)

Becky's Fresh Apple Cake

3 cups self-rising flour
1 teaspoon cinnamon
1½ cups vegetable oil
2 cups sugar
3 eggs

1 teaspoon vanilla extract
2–3 cups chopped peeled apples
1 cup chopped pecans
1 cup packed brown sugar
⅓–½ cup lemon juice

Sift flour and cinnamon together. Beat oil and sugar in mixer bowl. Beat in eggs 1 at a time. Stir in vanilla. Add flour mixture and apples alternately to sugar mixture, mixing well after each addition. Stir in pecans. Batter will be thick. Pour into greased and floured tube or Bundt pan. Bake at 350° for 1¼ hours. Cool in pan for several minutes. Invert onto serving plate. Mix brown sugar with lemon juice in bowl. Drizzle over warm cake. Yields 16 servings.

Imogene Davis, Birmingham Life Club (Book 3)

Allie's Coconut Cake

1 (18¼-ounce) package white
    cake mix
1 (14-ounce) can sweetened
    condensed milk
1 (14-ounce) can coconut milk

1 (8-ounce) container whipped
    topping
1 (12-ounce) package frozen
    fresh coconut, thawed

Prepare and bake cake mix using package directions for a 9x13-inch cake pan. Punch holes in top of cake while still hot. Pour condensed milk and coconut milk over cake. Let cake stand until completely cool. Spread whipped topping over top. Sprinkle with coconut. Cut into squares. Yields 15 servings.

Mary Ann Stanley, Mobile Council (Book 4)

Tropical Orange Cake

1 (18¼-ounce) package white
    cake mix
1 cup water
2 eggs
1 (14-ounce) can sweetened
    condensed milk, divided

2 teaspoons grated orange peel
1 (3-ounce) can flaked coconut
    (1⅓ cups), divided
¼ cup thawed frozen orange
    juice concentrate

Combine cake mix, water, eggs, ⅓ cup condensed milk, and orange peel in a mixing bowl. Beat at low speed until moistened. Beat at high speed 3 minutes. Stir in 1 cup coconut. Pour into a greased and floured 9x13-inch cake pan. Bake at 350° for 30 minutes. Cool in pan on wire rack. Combine remaining condensed milk, remaining coconut, and orange juice concentrate in a bowl; mix well. Spread over cool cake. Chill, covered, in refrigerator. Yields 15 servings.

Donna Jean Bowman, Birmingham South Cahaba Council
(Book 4)

Mandarin Orange Cake

1 (18¼-ounce) package butter
  recipe cake mix
1 (11-ounce) can Mandarin
  oranges, undrained

½ cup vegetable oil
4 eggs

Combine all ingredients and mix approximately 2 minutes. Bake at 350° about 30 minutes in a greased and floured 9x13-inch pan or 2 round cake pans.

ICING:

1 (6-ounce) box vanilla instant
  pudding
1 (20-ounce) can crushed
  pineapple, drained

1 (8-ounce) carton Cool Whip

While cake is baking, prepare Icing by mixing instant pudding and pineapple; then refrigerate. When cake is cool, add Cool Whip to pudding and pineapple mixture. Frost cake and refrigerate.

Holly Woodard, Riverchase Council (Book 1)

Strawberry Pecan Cake

1 (18¼-ounce) box white cake
  mix
1 (3-ounce) box strawberry
  Jell-O
1 cup Wesson oil

½ cup milk
4 eggs
1 cup frozen strawberries
1 cup flaked coconut (optional)
1 cup chopped pecans

Mix cake mix and Jell-O together dry. Add oil, milk, and eggs, one at a time. Use mixing instructions on back of cake mix box. Add remaining ingredients; bake in 3 greased and floured cake pans or 1 (9x13-inch) pan for approximately 25–30 minutes. Cool thoroughly before frosting.

FROSTING:

1 stick margarine, softened
1 (1-pound) box confectioners'
  sugar

½ cup strawberries, drained
½ cup chopped pecans
½ cup flaked coconut (optional)

Cream margarine and sugar; add remaining ingredients and spread on cooled cake.

Ladon S. Young, Birmingham Central Council (Book 1)

Strawberry Heaven Cake

2 (10-ounce) packages frozen
  strawberries, thawed
1 (18¼-ounce) package butter
  recipe cake mix
1 (3-ounce) package strawberry
  gelatin

1 cup boiling water
1 (14-ounce) can sweetened
  condensed milk
1 (12-ounce) carton whipped
  topping

Drain a small amount of strawberry juice for topping; set aside. Prepare and bake cake mix using package directions for 9x13-inch cake pan. Dissolve gelatin in boiling water in bowl. Add condensed milk and strawberries; mix well. Pierce holes in hot cake with handle of wooden spoon. Pour strawberry mixture over top. Cool completely. Combine whipped topping with reserved strawberry juice in bowl. Spread over cooled cake. Chill for 2 hours to overnight. Yields 15 servings.

Mrs. Jack E. Gentle, Sr., Opelika Life Club (Book 3)

Strawberry Shortcake

1 (18¼-ounce) package moist
  yellow cake mix
1¼ cups water
¼ cup nonfat vanilla yogurt

¾ cup egg substitute
1½ cups fat-free whipped
  topping
1½ cups sliced strawberries

Combine cake mix, water, yogurt, and egg substitute in a mixing bowl. Beat at low speed until moistened. Beat 2 minutes at high speed. Pour into a greased and floured 9x13-inch cake pan. Bake at 350° for 30–35 minutes or until a wooden pick inserted in center comes out clean. Cool completely in pan on wire rack. Cut into squares and place on serving plates. Top with whipped topping and strawberries. Yields 15 servings.

Gussie Evans, Mobile Council (Book 4)

Easy Blueberry Cake

1 (18¼-ounce) package white
  cake mix
1 (8-ounce) package cream
  cheese, softened
½ cup confectioners' sugar

½ cup sugar
1 (16-ounce) carton whipped
  topping
1 (21-ounce) can blueberry pie
  filling

Prepare and bake cake mix using package directions for 2 layers. Slice each layer horizontally into halves. Combine cream cheese, confectioners' sugar, and sugar in bowl; mix well. Fold in whipped topping. Spread each layer with cream cheese mixture and pie filling. Stack layers together. Spread top of cake with remaining cream cheese mixture. Chill until serving time. Yields 12 servings.

Doris Summersgill, Mobile Life Club (Book 3)

Blueberry Crunch Cake

1 (20-ounce) can crushed
  pineapple
3 cups blueberries
1 (18¼-ounce) package yellow
  cake mix

1 stick (or more) margarine,
  melted
½ cup sugar
1 cup chopped pecans

Spread undrained pineapple evenly in bottom of a lightly greased 9x13-inch baking pan. Sprinkle blueberries over pineapple. Sprinkle cake mix evenly over blueberries. Drizzle melted margarine over cake mix and spread evenly. Add a small amount of water, if desired. Sprinkle with sugar and pecans. Bake at 350° for 30–40 minutes or until golden brown. Yields 10 servings.

Shirley Crocker, Birmingham Life Club (Book 4)

Blackberry Wine Cake

1 (18¼-ounce) package white
  cake mix
1 (3-ounce) package blackberry
  gelatin
1 stick butter
1 cup confectioners' sugar
1 cup blackberry wine

Prepare cake mix using package directions, adding blackberry gelatin. Bake in Bundt pan using package directions. Melt butter in a saucepan. Add confectioner' sugar and wine and mix until smooth. Pierce top of hot cake with a knife. Pour sauce over top. Yields 16 servings.

Dilla Samuel, Gadsden Life Club (Book 4)

Punch Bowl Cake

1 (18¼-ounce) package butter
  recipe cake mix, cooked
  according to directions for
  2-layer cake
2 (3-ounce) boxes vanilla
  instant pudding, prepared
  according to directions (mix
  each box separately)
Flaked coconut (optional)
2 (21-ounce) cans strawberry pie
  filling (or flavor of choice)
2 (20-ounce) cans crushed
  pineapple, slightly drained
1 (12-ounce) carton Cool Whip
Cherries and chopped nuts for
  garnish

Crumble 1 layer of cake in punch bowl; spread ½ vanilla pudding over cake. Sprinkle some coconut, if desired; spread with ½ pie filling and ½ pineapple. Crumble remaining layer of cake and spread with remaining ingredients as before. Top with Cool Whip, cherries, and nuts. Refrigerate.

Debbie Jarvis, Birmingham Central Council (Book 2)

Dump Cake

1 (20-ounce) can crushed
  pineapple
1 (21-ounce) can cherry pie
  filling
1 (18¼-ounce) box yellow cake
  mix

¾ cup butter, melted
½ cup flaked coconut
1 cup chopped pecans

Dump pineapple and pie filling into bottom of greased oblong baking pan. Smooth out. Sprinkle cake mix evenly over this. Pour melted butter over, then sprinkle with coconut and pecans. Bake at 350° for 1 hour. Serve from pan.

Martha Cantrell, Birmingham East Council (Book 1)

Hot Fudge Sundae Cake

1½ cups all-purpose flour
1 cup sugar
3 tablespoons plus ⅓ cup
  baking cocoa, divided
2½ teaspoons baking powder
¼ teaspoon salt
3 tablespoons margarine,
  melted

¾ cup milk
1½ teaspoons vanilla extract
¼ teaspoon cinnamon
1 cup chopped pecans
1 cup packed brown sugar
2 cups hot water

Mix flour, sugar, 3 tablespoons cocoa, baking powder, and salt in ungreased 9x13-inch cake pan. Add margarine, milk, vanilla, and cinnamon; mix well with fork. Stir in pecans; spread evenly in pan. Sprinkle with brown sugar and remaining ⅓ cup baking cocoa. Pour hot water over top; do not stir. Bake at 350° for 30 minutes. Cake will form a fudge sauce in bottom of pan. Yields 15 servings.

Sammie DeLoach, Birmingham South Cahaba Council and
Glenda Neal, Birmingham South Cahaba Council (Book 3)

Hummingbird Cake

3 cups all-purpose flour
2 cups sugar
1 teaspoon salt
1 teaspoon baking soda
1 teaspoon cinnamon
3 eggs, beaten

1½ cups oil
1½ teaspoons vanilla
1 (8-ounce) can crushed
   pineapple, drained
2 cups chopped bananas
1 cup chopped nuts

Combine dry ingredients; add eggs and oil; stir by hand until well mixed. Add vanilla, pineapple, bananas, and nuts. Spoon batter into large greased and floured sheet pan. Bake at 350° for 40–45 minutes.

ICING:

1 (1-pound) box confectioners'
   sugar
½ cup margarine, softened
1 (8-ounce) package cream
   cheese, softened

1 teaspoon vanilla
1 cup chopped nuts

Combine sugar, margarine, cream cheese, and vanilla. Spread on cake and sprinkle with chopped nuts.

Freida Elkourie, Birmingham South Council (Book 1)

Italian Cream Cake

1 stick margarine, softened
½ cup shortening
2 cups sugar
5 eggs
2 cups all-purpose flour

1 teaspoon baking soda
1 cup buttermilk
1 tablespoon vanilla
1 (7-ounce) container flaked
  coconut

Cream margarine and shortening; add sugar and beat well. Add eggs, one at a time. Add flour and baking soda alternately with buttermilk to creamed mixture. Add vanilla and coconut. Pour into 3 (9-inch) greased and floured baking pans. Bake at 350° for 40 minutes.

CREAM CHEESE FROSTING:

1 (8-ounce) package cream
  cheese, softened
½ stick margarine, softened
1 (1-pound) box confectioners'
  sugar

1 tablespoon vanilla
1 cup chopped pecans

Beat cream cheese and margarine until smooth. Add sugar and vanilla. Beat until smooth; add nuts and beat 1 minute. Spread on each layer and side and top of cake.

Harold Busby, Mobile Council (Book 1)

1-2-3-4 Cake

1 cup all-purpose flour
1 stick margarine, softened
1 cup chopped nuts, divided
1 (8-ounce) package cream
  cheese, softened
1 cup powdered sugar
1 (12-ounce) carton Cool Whip,
  divided

1 (3-ounce) package lemon
  instant pudding mix
1 (3-ounce) package vanilla
  instant pudding mix
3 cups cold milk

LAYER 1:

Mix flour, margarine, and ½ cup nuts; pat in bottom of 9x13-inch pan. Bake 15 minutes at 350°, then cool in refrigerator.

LAYER 2:

Beat cream cheese till soft; add powdered sugar and ¾ carton Cool Whip. Whip until well blended. Add to Layer 1.

LAYER 3:

Mix both puddings with 3 cups of milk. Put on Layer 2.

LAYER 4:

Use remaining Cool Whip and top off with remaining chopped nuts.

Karen Crowe, Riverchase Council (Book 1)

Lane Cake

1½ cups butter or margarine, softened, divided
4 cups sugar, divided
3½ cups all-purpose flour
3 teaspoons baking powder
1 cup milk
2 teaspoons vanilla, divided
8 eggs, separated
1 cup chopped raisins
1 cup chopped nuts
1 cup flaked coconut
1 cup wine or bourbon

Cream 1 cup butter and 2 cups sugar together until fluffy and light. Sift flour with baking powder. Add flour mixture to creamed mixture alternately with milk; add 1 teaspoon vanilla. Fold in stiffly beaten egg whites. Spoon batter into 3 (9-inch) greased and floured layer cake pans; bake at 350° for 20–30 minutes or until cakes test done.

Beat egg yolks slightly. Add remaining sugar and butter; cook in double boiler until thick, stirring constantly. Add raisins, nuts, and coconut. Stir in remaining 1 teaspoon vanilla and wine. Spread filling thickly between layers of cake and on top and side.

Joyce Reavis, Decatur Council (Book 1)

No-Bake Cheesecake

1 (8-ounce) package cream
  cheese, softened
1 (14-ounce) can sweetened
  condensed milk

1 teaspoon vanilla extract
⅓ cup lemon juice
1 graham cracker cheesecake
  crust

Beat cream cheese in mixer bowl until fluffy. Add condensed milk gradually, beating constantly. Add vanilla and lemon juice; mix well. Spoon into crust. Chill for 2–3 hours. Yields 20 servings.

Charles Clark, Life Member, Decatur Council (Book 3)

Chocolate Chip Cheesecake

2 cups finely crushed chocolate
  sandwich cookies
¼ cup shortening, melted
3 (8-ounce) packages cream
  cheese, softened
1 (14-ounce) can sweetened
  condensed milk

3 eggs
2 teaspoons vanilla extract
1 cup miniature chocolate chips
1 teaspoon flour

Mix cookie crumbs and shortening in bowl. Press over bottom of 9-inch springform pan. Beat cream cheese in mixer bowl until light. Add condensed milk gradually, beating constantly until smooth. Beat in eggs and vanilla. Toss half the chocolate chips with flour in bowl. Fold into batter. Spoon into prepared pan; sprinkle with remaining chocolate chips. Bake at 350° for 55 minutes or until center is set. Cool to room temperature. Chill until serving time. Yields 12 servings.

Betty Foshee, Decatur Council (Book 3)

Chocolate Cheesecake

CRUST:

1½ cups graham cracker
  crumbs
2 tablespoons sugar

¼ teaspoon cinnamon
½ stick butter, melted

Combine first 3 ingredients in mixing bowl; mix well. Add butter and mix until mixture is crumbly. Press crumb mixture over the bottom and slightly up side of a springform pan.

CAKE:

1½ cups semisweet chocolate
  chips
2 eggs
1 cup sugar

1 cup sour cream
2 (8-ounce) packages cream
  cheese, softened
2 tablespoons melted butter

Melt chocolate chips in top of a double boiler over hot water, stirring until smooth. Set melted chocolate aside. Combine eggs, sugar, and sour cream in mixing bowl. Beat for 1 minute or until smooth and well blended. Add melted chocolate gradually, beating constantly. Beat in cream cheese and butter gradually, beating constantly until well blended. Pour cream cheese mixture into prepared Crust. Bake at 325° for 45 minutes or until cheesecake is set in center. Let stand at room temperature for 1 hour or longer to cool. Chill in refrigerator for 6 hours or longer. Loosen cheesecake from side of pan. Remove side of pan. Serve with whipped cream, if desired. Yields 10–12 servings.

Variation: May substitute 2 crust-lined pie plates for springform pan and bake for 35 minutes or until centers are set.

Betty Darnell, Gadsden Life Club (Book 4)

Southern Gingerbread

2½ cups all-purpose flour
2 teaspoons baking soda
½ teaspoon baking powder
1½ teaspoons cinnamon
1 teaspoon ginger
½ teaspoon ground cloves

½ teaspoon allspice
¾ cup packed brown sugar
¾ cup molasses
¾ cup shortening, melted
2 eggs, beaten
1 cup boiling water

Sift flour, baking soda, baking powder, cinnamon, ginger, cloves, and allspice together. Combine brown sugar, molasses, and shortening in a bowl; mix well. Add eggs; mix well. Stir in flour mixture. Add water; mix well. Pour into 2 greased and floured 8x8-inch cake pans. Bake at 350° for 30–40 minutes or until cake tests done. Serve with lemon sauce or applesauce. Yields 2 cakes.

Althea Dunn, Bon Secour Life Club (Book 4)

Milk Chocolate Frosting

1½ cups sugar
1 cup evaporated milk,
  undiluted
½ cup butter, melted

1 (6-ounce) package semisweet
  chocolate pieces
1 cup marshmallow crème
2 tablespoons milk

Combine sugar, evaporated milk, and butter in a heavy saucepan; cook over medium heat until mixture reaches soft-ball stage (237°). Remove from heat; add chocolate pieces and marshmallow crème, stirring until melted. Add milk and stir until smooth. Yields frosting for 1 (10-inch) cake.

Opal Mofitt, Tuscaloosa Pioneer Unit (Book 1)

Cookies and Candies

1968
Trimline

The twelve-button Touch-Tone Trimline was dramatically different from any other phone at the time. With the first ever dial-in-handset, it allowed people to dial a new call without returning to the base of the phone. The design of the phone later paved the way for today's cordless and cellular phones. Although only ten buttons were needed for ordinary dialing, the two "extra" buttons (the * and # keys) were added for advanced services and for dialing international phone calls. The first Touch-Tone Trimline phone had round buttons instead of square. The convenience of having the dial in the handset was especially handy in the wall-mount model. The Trimline model also introduced the concept of modular plugs. Also in 1968, 911 was introduced as a nationwide emergency number.

Graham Cracker Cookies

1 box graham crackers
1 stick butter
1 stick margarine

¼ cup brown sugar
¼ cup white sugar
1 cup chopped pecans

In a 9x13-inch pan, place a single layer of crackers. In a saucepan, melt butter and margarine; add sugar and bring to a boil. Boil 2 minutes. Add pecans. Pour over graham crackers. Bake at 350° for 8 minutes. Remove from oven; let cool. Break into pieces.

Mary Alice Neal, Riverchase Council (Book 2)

Easy Fruitcake Cookies

1 pound mixed candied fruit,
  chopped
½ cup all-purpose flour
Salt to taste

1 (4-ounce) can flaked coconut
2 cups chopped pecans
1 (14-ounce) can sweetened
  condensed milk

Dredge candied fruit in flour. Combine fruit, salt, coconut, and pecans in bowl; mix well. Add condensed milk, stirring until combined. Drop by spoonfuls onto greased cookie sheet. Bake at 275° for 25–30 minutes or until brown. Remove to wire rack to cool. Store in airtight container 5 days before serving. May substitute self-rising flour for all-purpose flour. Yields 48 servings.

Trudy B. McCann, Huntsville Council (Book 3)

Fruit Cookies

1 cup brown sugar
1 stick margarine, softened
2 eggs
1½ teaspoons baking soda, dissolved in 1½ tablespoons milk
⅓ cup whiskey or brandy
1½ cups all-purpose flour, sifted
½ teaspoon cinnamon
½ teaspoon cloves
½ teaspoon nutmeg
½ pound candied cherries
½ pound candied pineapple
3 cups chopped pecans
1 (1½-ounce) box white raisins

Mix thoroughly; drop onto cookie sheet and bake at 300° for 20 minutes.

Note: Mix a little flour with candied fruits to keep them from sinking to bottom.

Bonnie Summers, Huntsville Council (Book 1)

Forgotten Cookies

These are beautiful cookies. They are lovely for teas or receptions.

2 egg whites, at room temperature
¼ teaspoon cream of tartar
⅛ teaspoon salt
⅔ cup sugar
1 teaspoon vanilla extract
1 (6-ounce) package miniature chocolate chips
1 cup broken pecans

Preheat oven to 350°. Beat egg whites and cream of tartar. Add sugar gradually and beat until sugar is dissolved. Add remaining ingredients. Drop by teaspoonfuls on foil-lined cookie sheets. Place all cookies in oven at one time. When you place cookies in preheated oven, turn off heat immediately and leave overnight to dry out. In other words, "forget" about them until morning. Remove with spatula. Makes about 5 dozen.

Jann LeCroy, Birmingham Central Council (Book 1)

Hello Dolly Cookies

1 stick butter, melted
1 cup graham cracker crumbs
1 cup chocolate chips
1 cup butterscotch chips

1 cup chopped pecans
1 cup flaked coconut
1 (14-ounce) can sweetened
 condensed milk

Melt butter in a 9x13-inch pan, then layer ingredients in pan as follows: crumbs, chips, nuts, and coconut. Drizzle milk over all. Do not stir. Bake at 350° for 30 minutes. Cool and cut into squares.

Rosemary Parker, Birmingham Central Council (Book 2)

Peanut Butter Cookies

1 cup shortening
1 cup packed brown sugar
1 cup sugar
2 eggs
1 teaspoon vanilla extract

1 cup peanut butter
2½ cups all-purpose flour
½ teaspoon salt
2 teaspoons baking soda

Cream shortening, brown sugar, sugar, eggs, and vanilla in mixer bowl until light and fluffy. Add peanut butter. Add mixture of flour, salt, and baking soda; mix well. Drop by rounded teaspoonfuls onto ungreased cookie sheet. Bake at 350° for 10 minutes. Yields 48 servings.

Gail Perez, Huntsville Council (Book 3)

Mud Cookies

2 cups sugar
½ stick margarine
¼ cup baking cocoa
½ cup milk

3 cups quick-cooking oats
½ cup peanut butter
1 teaspoon vanilla extract

Combine sugar, margarine, baking cocoa, and milk in a saucepan. Bring to a boil. Boil for 1 minute, stirring constantly. Add oats, peanut butter, and vanilla; mix well. Drop by spoonfuls onto a nonstick cookie sheet. Chill, covered, in refrigerator until firm. Yields 2 dozen.

Jeanette Norton, Shoals Life Club (Book 4)

Neiman Marcus Cookies

5 cups rolled oats
4 sticks butter, softened
2 cups sugar
2 cups packed brown sugar
4 eggs
2 teaspoons vanilla extract
4 cups all-purpose flour

1 teaspoon salt
2 teaspoons baking powder
2 teaspoons baking soda
4 cups chocolate chips
1 (8-ounce) milk chocolate bar, grated
3 cups chopped nuts

Process oats in a blender to a fine powder. Cream butter, sugar, and brown sugar in mixing bowl until light and fluffy. Add eggs and vanilla; mix well. Combine flour, ground oats, salt, baking powder, and baking soda in a bowl; mix well. Add to creamed mixture; mix well. Stir in chocolate chips, chocolate bar, and nuts. Roll into balls. Place 2 inches apart on cookie sheets. Bake at 375° for 10 minutes. Cool on wire racks. Yields 9 dozen.

Sara Cooley, Birmingham Life Club (Book 4)

Chocolate Chip Cookies

1 stick butter, softened
1½ cups packed brown sugar
2 eggs
1 teaspoon vanilla extract

2⅔ cups baking mix
2 cups chocolate chips
½ cup (or more) chopped nuts

Cream butter and brown sugar in a mixing bowl until light and fluffy. Beat in eggs 1 at a time. Stir in vanilla. Add baking mix gradually, mixing with a wooden spoon. Fold in chocolate chips and nuts. Drop by spoonfuls onto greased cookie sheets. Bake at 375° for 8–10 minutes or until brown. Cool on wire racks. Yields 2½–3 dozen.

Mabel Smartt, Decatur Council (Book 4)

Orange Slice Cookies

½ (18¼-ounce) box yellow
   cake mix
1 egg

⅓ (scant) cup vegetable oil
11 orange candy slices, chopped
1 cup chopped nuts

Combine ½ cake mix, egg, oil, orange slice pieces, and nuts in a mixing bowl; mix well. Drop by teaspoonfuls onto ungreased cookie sheets. Bake at 350° for 10 minutes. Cool on wire racks. Yields 2 dozen.

Virginia Killian, Gadsden Life Club (Book 4)

Magic Cookie Bars

½ cup butter, melted
1½ cups graham cracker
  crumbs
1⅓ cups sweetened condensed
  milk

1 cup chopped walnuts
1 cup chocolate chips
1⅓ cups flaked coconut

Coat bottom of 9x13-inch baking pan with melted butter. Layer graham cracker crumbs, condensed milk, walnuts, chocolate chips, and coconut in order listed in prepared pan. Bake at 350° for 25 minutes or until light brown. Remove to wire rack to cool. Cut into bars. Yields 36 servings.

Ethel Beasley, Birmingham Life Club (Book 3)

Gooey Butter Bars

1 stick margarine, melted
1 (18¼-ounce) box butter
  cake mix
3 eggs, divided

3 cups confectioners' sugar
1 stick margarine, softened
1 (8-ounce) package cream
  cheese, softened

Combine melted margarine, cake mix, and 1 egg in a bowl; mix well. Spread over bottom of a nonstick 9x13-inch baking pan. Combine confectioners' sugar, softened margarine, cream cheese, and remaining 2 eggs in a bowl; mix well. Spread over crust. Bake at 350° for 30–40 minutes or until brown. Let stand until cool. Cut into bars. Yields 2 dozen.

Debby Sims, Gadsden Life Club (Book 4)

Polly Jones' Apple Bars

3 eggs, beaten
2 cups sugar
1 cup vegetable oil
2 cups all-purpose flour
½ teaspoon salt

1 teaspoon cinnamon
2 cups chopped peeled apples
Chopped nuts to taste
Confectioners' sugar to taste

Beat eggs, sugar, and oil in a mixing bowl until well combined. Add flour, salt, and cinnamon; mix well. Fold in apples and nuts. Pour into a greased and floured 9x13-inch baking pan. Bake at 350° for 40–45 minutes or until brown. Sprinkle with confectioners' sugar while warm. Let stand until cool. Cut into bars. Yields 2 dozen.

Kitty Logan Brown, Gadsden Life Council (Book 4)

 The first Picturephone test system, built in 1956, was crude—it transmitted an image only once every two seconds. By 1964 a complete experimental system, the "Mod 1," had been developed, but failed miserably. It wasn't until decades later, with improvements in speed, resolution, miniaturization, and the incorporation of Picturephone into another piece of desktop equipment, the computer, that the promise of a personal video communication system was realized.

Brownies

2 cups sugar
2 cups sifted all-purpose flour
1 stick butter
½ cup Crisco oil
3 heaping tablespoons cocoa

1 cup water
½ teaspoon baking soda
1 teaspoon vanilla
2 eggs
½ cup buttermilk

Mix together sugar and flour; set aside. In saucepan, combine butter, oil, cocoa, and water; bring to a boil; pour over sugar and flour mixture. Add soda, vanilla, eggs, and buttermilk. Mix well; pour into a greased and floured 9x13-inch pan. Bake 1 hour at 300°.

ICING:

1 stick margarine
3 heaping tablespoons cocoa
6 tablespoons buttermilk
1 (1-pound) box confectioners'
sugar

1 teaspoon vanilla
½ cup chopped nuts

In saucepan, combine margarine, cocoa, and buttermilk; bring to a boil. Remove from heat. Add confectioners' sugar, vanilla, and nuts; mix well and pour over cake while still hot.

Rosemary Parker, Birmingham Central Council (Book 2)

Caramel Brownies

2 cups baking mix
1 (1-pound) package light
  brown sugar

4 eggs
1 cup chopped nuts
1 teaspoon vanilla extract

Combine baking mix and brown sugar in mixing bowl; mix well. Beat in eggs until well blended. Add nuts and vanilla; mix well. Pour mixture into a greased 9x13-inch baking pan. Bake at 325° for 25 minutes or until firm in center. Let stand until cool. Cut into bars. Yields 2 dozen.

Sue Small, Selma Life Club (Book 4)

Old-Fashioned Tea Cakes

1 cup shortening
1 cup sugar
1 egg, beaten
2 tablespoons buttermilk
2½ cups (or more) all-purpose
  flour

¼ teaspoon salt
2 teaspoons baking powder
1 teaspoon vanilla extract

Beat shortening in a mixing bowl at low speed. Add sugar, egg, and buttermilk; mix well. Sift flour, salt, and baking powder together. Add to sugar mixture; mix well. Add vanilla; mix well. Roll dough ¼ inch thick on a floured surface. Cut with cookie cutter. Place on nonstick cookie sheets. Bake at 350° for 8 minutes. Cool on wire racks. Yields 3 dozen.

Hazel Campbell, Birmingham Life Club (Book 4)

Coconut Igloos

Delicious and easy to make.

1 stick butter (no substitute)
1 cup sugar
1 (20-ounce) can crushed
  pineapple, drained
1 cup dark raisins, finely
  chopped

1 cup chopped pecans
2 (8-ounce) boxes butter cookies
1 pint whipping cream, whipped
1 (7-ounce) can grated coconut

Cream butter and sugar; add pineapple, raisins, and nuts. Mix well. Spread between 3 cookies to make base for each igloo. Allow cookies and fruit mixture to stand at room temperature 8 hours. Sweeten whipped cream to taste (may add a little vanilla). Frost top and sides with whipped cream to resemble an igloo; sprinkle with coconut. Place in refrigerator until time to serve. Makes approximately 18–20. May be frozen.

Anethia Avery Reliford, Riverchase Council (Book 2)

Quick and Easy Low-Fat Date Log

2½ cups sugar
1 cup milk
1 (16-ounce) package dates

1 cup chopped pecans
1 tablespoon vanilla extract

Bring sugar and milk to a boil in saucepan, stirring frequently. Stir in chopped dates. Cook until thickened, stirring constantly. Remove from heat, beating until of desired consistency. Add pecans and vanilla; mix well. Pour mixture on damp towel; shape into log. Cool before slicing. Yields 12 servings.

Betty Smith, Mobile Life Club (Book 3)

Vanilla Nut Roll

1 (14-ounce) can sweetened
  condensed milk
1 cup flaked coconut
2 cups chopped pecans

½ package vanilla wafers,
  crushed
Confectioners' sugar to taste

Combine condensed milk, coconut, pecans, and vanilla wafer crumbs in a bowl; mix well. Divide mixture into 2 or 3 equal portions. Roll each portion into a log and coat with confectioners' sugar. Chill, covered, in refrigerator. Cut into slices. You may press mixture into a square pan and sprinkle with confectioners' sugar, if desired. Yields 2–2½ pounds.

Oneida C. Allen, Tuscaloosa Council (Book 4)

Church Windows

1 (12-ounce) package semisweet
  chocolate chips
1 stick margarine
1 cup chopped pecans

1 bag colored miniature
  marshmallows
1 (7-ounce) can flaked coconut

Melt chocolate chips and margarine; cool. Pour mixture over nuts and marshmallows. Mix well. Divide into 4 equal parts. Put on 4 pieces of wax paper; pat together with hands. Make 4 rolls. Sprinkle coconut over rolls; roll in wax paper. Refrigerate 2 hours and slice.

Hazel Campbell, Birmingham South Council (Book 1)

Chip Balls

1 cup butter, softened
½ cup granulated sugar
1 egg yolk
1 teaspoon vanilla
2½ cups sifted all-purpose
   flour
½ cup crumbled potato chips

½ cup chopped walnuts or
   pecans
½ cup semisweet chocolate
   pieces
Granulated or powdered sugar
   for sprinkling on top

Heat oven to 325°. With mixer, cream butter, sugar, egg yolk, and vanilla till fluffy. At low speed, mix in flour, about ½ at a time, till smooth. Add potato chips and nuts. Shape into 1-inch balls, pressing 2 or 3 chocolate chips into each. Place on greased cookie sheet. Bake for 25 minutes. Sprinkle with granulated sugar or confectioners' sugar as soon as taken out of oven. Yields 2–4 dozen.

Mary Alice Neal, Riverchase Council (Book 2)

Date-Rice Krispies Balls

1 stick margarine
1 cup sugar
1 (8-ounce) package chopped
   dates

1 cup chopped nuts
2½ cups Rice Krispies
Powdered sugar

Combine margarine, sugar, and dates in saucepan. Cook over medium-high heat until dates dissolve and melt, stirring constantly. Add nuts. Pour mixture over Rice Krispies, which are in a large bowl. Mix together. While warm, roll into small balls and roll in powdered sugar.

Hazel Campbell, Birmingham South Council (Book 1)

Buckeye Balls

1½ cups creamy peanut butter
½ cup lightly salted butter or
  margarine, softened
1 teaspoon vanilla extract
1 (1-pound) package
  confectioners' sugar

1 (6-ounce) package semisweet
  chocolate pieces
1 tablespoon solid vegetable
  shortening

Line baking sheet with wax paper. In a medium bowl, mix peanut butter, butter, vanilla, and sugar with hands to form a smooth dough. Mixture will be very stiff. Shape dough into balls using 2 teaspoons for each. Place on wax paper and put in refrigerator.

In the top of a double boiler over simmering—not boiling—water, melt chocolate and shortening together. When smooth, pour into a small bowl or measuring cup. Remove peanut butter balls from refrigerator. Insert a wooden toothpick into ball and dip into melted chocolate so that ¾ of ball is covered. Return to wax paper, chocolate side down, and remove pick. Repeat with all balls. Refrigerate on wax paper 30 minutes or longer, until chocolate is firm, not sticky. To store, remove balls from wax paper and place in plastic containers, with wax paper between layers. Makes about 5 dozen candies.

Mary Ann Davis, Anniston Council (Book 1)

Chocolate Candy

5 cups sugar
1 (12-ounce) can evaporated
  milk
2 sticks butter
1 (12-ounce) package chocolate
  chips

1 (7-ounce) jar marshmallow
  crème
1 teaspoon vanilla
Chopped nuts (optional)

Combine sugar, evaporated milk, and butter in a heavy metal saucepan; bring to a boil over medium heat. Leave heat setting at medium and continue to cook for 10 minutes. Remove from heat and add chocolate chips, marshmallow crème, and vanilla; stir until smooth and creamy. Pour into large buttered pan to cool. Nuts may be added or placed on top.

Betty W. Sanders, President, Birmingham Central Council
(Book 1)

Pecan Clusters

5 cups sugar
1 stick butter
1 (12-ounce) can evaporated
  milk
½ teaspoon salt

4 cups pecan halves
1½ pounds chocolate kisses,
  peeled
1 (9-ounce) jar marshmallow
  crème

Combine sugar, butter, milk, and salt in saucepan; boil 7 minutes, stirring constantly. Remove from heat. Add nuts, chocolate kisses, and marshmallow crème. Mix well. Drop on wax paper. Makes about 6 pounds candy.

Patti Smith and Peggy Hunter, Anniston Council (Book 1)

Toasted Pecan Clusters

3 cups pecan pieces
3 tablespoons butter or
  margarine, melted

12 ounces chocolate candy
  coating

Combine pecans and butter in a 10x15-inch baking pan. Bake at 300° for 20 minutes, stirring after 10 minutes. Melt chocolate in a heavy saucepan over low heat. Remove from heat. Cool 2 minutes. Stir in toasted pecans. Drop by rounded teaspoons onto wax paper. Let stand until cool   Yields 1½ pounds.

Faith Kirby Richardson, Gadsden Life Club (Book 4)

Texas Millionaires

1 package Kraft caramels
1 tablespoon milk
2 cups pecan pieces
1 teaspoon vanilla flavoring

1 (12-ounce) package milk
  chocolate morsels
½ bar paraffin

Melt caramels and milk in top of double boiler. Add pecan pieces and vanilla. Mix well. Drop on greased wax paper. Let stand until cool. While caramels are cooling, melt together in top of double boiler the chocolate morsels and paraffin. Using 2 forks, dip caramels in chocolate. Drop on wax paper to cool.

Judy Robertson, Riverchase Council (Book 2)

Gooey Turtles

1 stick butter, melted
1½ cups vanilla wafer crumbs
2 cups semisweet chocolate
  chips

1 cup chopped pecans
1 (12-ounce) jar caramel topping

Combine butter and vanilla wafer crumbs in a 9x13-inch baking pan; mix well. Press crumb mixture evenly over bottom of pan. Sprinkle with chocolate chips and pecans. Remove lid from caramel topping, and microwave on HIGH for 1–1½ minutes or until hot, stirring after 30 seconds. Drizzle topping over pecans. Bake at 350° for 12–15 minutes or until chocolate chips are melted. Cool in pan on a wire rack. Chill, covered, in refrigerator 30 minutes. Cut into bars. You may use reduced-fat vanilla wafers, chocolate chips, and caramel topping. Yields 2½ pounds.

Jo Ann Thomas, Selma Life Club (Book 4)

Mistake-Free Fudge

2 cups semisweet chocolate
  chips
1 (14-ounce) can sweetened
  condensed milk

1 teaspoon vanilla extract
1 cup chopped pecans

Combine chocolate chips and condensed milk in saucepan. Cook over low heat until blended, stirring constantly. Remove from heat. Stir in vanilla and pecans. Spoon into wax-paper-lined dish. Chill until firm. Cut into squares. Yields 48 servings.

Lyn Jordan, Montgomery Council (Book 3)

Willa's Sour Cream Fudge

2 cups sugar
1 cup sour cream
¼ teaspoon vinegar
2 tablespoons light corn syrup

Salt to taste
2 tablespoons margarine
1 cup chopped pecans

Combine sugar, sour cream, vinegar, corn syrup, and salt in saucepan; mix well. Cook over medium heat to 234°–240° on candy thermometer, soft-ball stage, stirring constantly. Remove from heat. Stir in margarine and pecans. Cool slightly. Stir until of desired consistency. Pour into buttered dish or drop by spoonfuls onto wax paper. Yields 24 servings.

Jane Knox, Montgomery Life Club (Book 3)

Microwave Fudge with Pecans

1 (1-pound) package
  confectioners' sugar
1½ tablespoons baking cocoa
1 stick butter, melted

¼ cup evaporated milk
1 teaspoon vanilla extract
Chopped pecans

Combine confectioners' sugar and baking cocoa in a microwave-safe bowl and mix well. Add butter and mix until creamy. Stir in milk. Microwave on HIGH 2 minutes. Add vanilla and pecans; mix well. Spoon mixture into a greased pan. Cool in pan several minutes. Chill, covered, in refrigerator until firm. Cut into squares. Yields 1¼ pounds.

Pam Dyer, Riverchase Council (Book 4)

Microwave Peanut Brittle

1 cup raw peanuts
1 cup sugar
½ cup light corn syrup
Pinch of salt

1 teaspoon butter or margarine
1 teaspoon vanilla extract
1 teaspoon baking soda

Combine peanuts, sugar, corn syrup, and salt in a microwave-safe 1½-quart dish; mix well. Microwave on HIGH 7–8 minutes, stirring after 4 minutes. Blend in butter and vanilla. Microwave 2 minutes. Stir in baking soda gently until mixture is light and foamy. Pour mixture onto a greased baking sheet and spread thinly. Let stand 30 minutes to 1 hour or until cool. Break into pieces. Yields 1 pound.

Adeline Neal, Birmingham Life Club (Book 4)

New Orleans Pralines

2 cups sugar
½ cup packed brown sugar
¾ cup evaporated milk

1 tablespoon corn syrup .
Salt to taste
2 cups pecans

Combine sugar, brown sugar, evaporated milk, corn syrup, salt, and pecans in saucepan, stirring until sugars dissolve. Cook over medium heat to 234°–240° on candy thermometer, soft-ball stage, stirring constantly. Remove from heat. Beat until thickened. Drop by spoonfuls onto wax paper. Let stand until set. Yields 32 servings.

Ida Skidmore, Shoals Life Club (Book 3)

Delicious Buttermilk Pralines

1 cup buttermilk	1 teaspoon vanilla extract
2 cups sugar	1 tablespoon butter
1 teaspoon baking soda	2 cups pecans

Stir buttermilk, sugar, and baking soda in saucepan until sugar dissolves. Cook over medium heat to 234°–240° on candy thermometer, soft-ball stage, stirring constantly. Stir in vanilla, butter, and pecans. Beat until mixture is thick and glossy. Drop by spoonfuls onto buttered wax paper. Store in airtight container. Yields 40 servings.

Jane G. Patterson, Decatur Council (Book 3)

Pies and Other Desserts

1980
Cordless

Cordless phones first appeared around 1980 and were primitive by today's standards. These phones, without cables or cords, chiefly used radio frequency and were initially given a frequency of 27 MHz by the Federal Communications Commission (FCC), which is the same frequency range used by CB radio. The base needs a separate power source to transmit the signal to the handset. The cordless handset is powered by a battery that is recharged by the base station. By 1998 Caller ID was introduced, 2.4 GHz frequencies opened, and a Digital Spread Spectrum signal became available. This added security and spread the signal 360 degrees from the base to the handset, so there were no dead spots and distance could go to a quarter mile. As additional features were added, prices dropped and demand rose. Consumers now wanted all their phones to be cordless. This created a new set of problems. If there was ever a power failure, you wouldn't have any working phones.

Peanut Butter Pie

1 (8-ounce) package cream
cheese, softened
1 cup crunchy peanut butter
1½ cups sifted powdered sugar
1 (16-ounce) carton Cool Whip

2 (9-inch) graham cracker
crusts
Chocolate chips or chocolate
shavings (optional)

Combine cream cheese and peanut butter in a large bowl; beat at medium speed until light and fluffy. Add powdered sugar and Cool Whip. Beat until smooth. Pour into crusts; freeze for 8 hours or overnight. You may decorate with chocolate chips or chocolate shavings, if desired.

Mary Caddell, Tuscaloosa Life Member Club (Book 2)

Easy Peanut Butter Pie

⅓ cup peanut butter
1 (3-ounce) package cream
cheese, softened
1 (16-ounce) carton whipped
topping

1 (9-inch) graham cracker pie
shell

Combine peanut butter, cream cheese, and whipped topping in bowl; mix well. Spoon into pie shell. Chill until serving time. Yields 8 servings.

Charles Clark, Life Member, Decatur Council (Book 3)

Chocolate Pie

1⅓ cups sugar, divided
⅛ teaspoon salt
¼ cup cornstarch
5 tablespoons baking cocoa
4 eggs, separated

2 cups milk
½ stick margarine
1 (9-inch) pie shell, baked
¼ teaspoon cream of tartar

Combine 1 cup sugar, salt, cornstarch, cocoa, lightly beaten egg yolks, milk, and margarine in a double boiler. Cook until thickened, stirring constantly. Pour into pie shell. Beat egg whites with cream of tartar in mixing bowl until soft peaks form. Add remaining ⅓ cup sugar gradually, beating constantly until stiff peaks form. Spoon over pie filling, sealing to edge. Bake at 350° or broil until meringue is light golden brown. Yields 6–8 servings.

Kathryn Morgan, Gadsden Life Club (Book 4)

Hershey Bar Pie

1 (7-ounce) Hershey's chocolate
    bar with almonds
1 (12-ounce) container whipped
    topping, divided

1 (9-inch) pie shell, baked

Grate candy bar, grating around almonds and leaving almonds intact. Reserve 1 tablespoon grated chocolate. Combine remaining grated chocolate, ¾ of the whipped topping, and almonds in a bowl; mix well. Pour into pie shell. Spread remaining whipped topping over top. Sprinkle with reserved grated chocolate. Chill until serving time. Yields 6–8 servings.

Mary Alice Neal, Birmingham Life Club (Book 4)

Chocolate Fudge Pies

3 cups sugar
⅛ teaspoon salt
7 tablespoons baking cocoa
1 (12-ounce) can evaporated
    milk
1 cup chopped pecans

½ cup butter, melted
4 eggs, beaten
1 teaspoon vanilla extract
3 (9-inch) pie shells, unbaked
Whipped cream or ice cream

Combine sugar, salt, and cocoa in bowl; mix well with wooden spoon. Stir in evaporated milk. Add pecans and butter; mix well. Beat in eggs and vanilla. Pour evenly into pie shells. Bake at 350° for 40 minutes. Serve with whipped cream or ice cream. Yields 24 servings.

Sandra McKinney, Birmingham Metro Council (Book 3)

Fudge Pie

1 stick butter or margarine
2 squares unsweetened
    chocolate
1 cup sugar
2 eggs, lightly beaten

½ cup all-purpose flour
¼ teaspoon salt
1 tablespoon vanilla extract
½ cup chopped pecans

Combine butter and chocolate in a saucepan. Heat over low heat until melted. Add sugar and eggs; mix well. Add flour, salt, and vanilla; mix well. Stir in pecans. Pour into a greased pie plate. Bake at 325° for 25 minutes. Yields 6–8 servings.

Note: You may substitute 6 tablespoons baking cocoa plus 2 tablespoons vegetable oil for the unsweetened chocolate.

D. Christine Kirkley, Birmingham Life Club (Book 4)

Cream Cheese Brownie Pie

1 refrigerator pie pastry
1 (8-ounce) package cream
  cheese, softened
3 tablespoons sugar
1 teaspoon vanilla
3 eggs, divided

1 (15-ounce) package Thick 'n'
  Fudgy Hot Fudge Swirl Deluxe
  Brownie Mix
¼ cup vegetable oil
2 tablespoons water, divided
½ cup chopped pecans

Fit pastry into pie plate and trim the edge. Combine cream cheese, sugar, vanilla, and 1 egg in a mixing bowl and beat until smooth; set aside. Set aside the hot fudge packet from the brownie mix. Combine brownie mix, vegetable oil, 1 tablespoon water, and remaining 2 eggs in a large bowl. Beat 50 strokes with a spoon. Spread ½ cup of mixture in pastry-lined pie plate. Top with cream cheese mixture, spreading gently. Spread remaining brownie mixture over top. Sprinkle with pecans. Bake at 350° for 40–50 minutes or until center is puffed and crust is golden brown.

Place hot fudge from packet in small, microwave-safe bowl. Microwave on HIGH for 30 seconds. Stir in remaining 1 tablespoon water. Drizzle hot fudge over pie. Let stand 3 hours or until cooled completely. Chill until serving time. Yields 6–8 servings.

Narice Sutton, Birmingham Life Club (Book 4)

Quick and Easy Pecan Pie

½ cup butter, melted
1 cup pecans
1 cup light brown sugar
½ cup white sugar
1 heaping tablespoon flour

2 eggs
2–3 teaspoons milk
1 teaspoon vanilla
1 (9-inch) pie shell, unbaked

Combine all ingredients; pour into unbaked pie shell. Bake at 350°
for 35 minutes; lower oven temperature to 250° and bake an additional 30 minutes.

Darlene Day, Decatur Council (Book 1)

Old-Fashioned Pecan Pie

1 cup sugar
½ stick butter, softened
⅔ cup corn syrup
1 tablespoon flour
¼ teaspoon salt

3 eggs, lightly beaten
1 teaspoon vanilla extract
1 cup chopped pecans
1 deep-dish pie shell, unbaked

Combine sugar, butter, and corn syrup in a bowl; blend well. Add
flour, salt, and eggs; mix well. Stir in vanilla and pecans. Pour into
pie shell. Bake at 350° for 1 hour. The filling recipe can be doubled
to make 3 shallower pies. Yields 6–8 servings.

Doris B. Thrasher, Gadsden Life Club (Book 4)

Pecan Cheese Pie

⅓ cup plus ¼ cup sugar, divided
1 (8-ounce) package cream cheese, softened
4 eggs, beaten, divided
2 teaspoons vanilla, divided
¼ teaspoon salt
1 (9-inch) pie shell, unbaked
1½ cups chopped pecans
1 cup light corn syrup

Cream ⅓ cup sugar and cream cheese in a mixing bowl until light and fluffy. Add 1 egg, 1 teaspoon vanilla, and salt; mix well. Pour into pie shell. Sprinkle with pecans. Combine corn syrup, remaining ¼ cup sugar, remaining 3 eggs, and remaining 1 teaspoon vanilla in a bowl; mix well. Pour over cream cheese mixture. Bake at 375° for 35–40 minutes or until set. Cool completely. Chill until serving time. Yields 6–8 servings.

Narice Sutton, Birmingham Life Club (Book 4)

Heavenly Pie

1 (8-ounce) package cream cheese, softened
1 (14-ounce) can sweetened condensed milk
⅓ cup lemon juice
1 (9-ounce) carton frozen whipped topping, thawed
½ cup chopped pecans
1 cup fruit, drained (pineapple, peaches, or fruit cocktail)
2 (9-inch) graham cracker pie shells

Combine cream cheese, condensed milk, and lemon juice; beat until smooth. Fold in whipped topping; stir in pecans and fruit. Pour into pie shells and refrigerate for several hours. Yields 2 (9-inch) pies.

Faith Kirby, Anniston Council (Book 1)

Lemonade Pie

1 (14-ounce) can sweetened
  condensed milk
1 (6-ounce) can frozen
  lemonade

1 (12-ounce) carton Cool Whip
Juice of ½ lemon
2 (9-inch) graham cracker
  pie shells

Mix first 4 ingredients and pour into pie shells. Refrigerate at least 1 hour before serving.

Linda Sammons, Birmingham South Council (Book 1)

Luscious Lemon Pie

1 (14-ounce) can sweetened
  condensed milk
1 (21-ounce) can lemon pie
  filling
½ cup (or more) lemon juice

1 (9-inch) graham cracker pie
  shell
1 (8-ounce) carton whipped
  topping

Combine condensed milk, pie filling, and lemon juice in bowl; mix well. Spoon into pie shell. Spread with whipped topping. Freeze until firm. Let stand at room temperature 2–3 hours (or until thawed) before serving. Yields 8 servings.

Frances Coleman, Huntsville Life Club (Book 3)

Million Dollar Pie

1 (8-ounce) carton Cool Whip
¼ cup lemon juice
1 (14-ounce) can sweetened
  condensed milk
1 cup crushed pineapple,
  drained

1 cup chopped nuts
½ cup chopped cherries
2 (9-inch) graham cracker
  crusts

Mix Cool Whip, lemon juice, and condensed milk; add pineapple, nuts, and cherries. Pour into 2 pie crusts. Refrigerate.

Frances Crenshaw, Birmingham East Council (Book 1)

Southern Apple Pie

1 recipe (2-crust) pie pastry
6 medium Granny Smith
  apples, peeled, cored, sliced
1 cup plus ½ teaspoon sugar,
  divided

2 tablespoons cornstarch
2 teaspoons vanilla extract
½ teaspoon cinnamon, divided
2 teaspoons margarine
1 tablespoon milk

Fit half the pastry into a 9-inch pie plate. Combine apples, 1 cup sugar, cornstarch, vanilla, and ¼ teaspoon cinnamon in bowl, tossing to coat apples. Spoon into pie plate. Dot with margarine. Top with remaining pastry, sealing edge and cutting vents. Brush with milk. Sprinkle with mixture of remaining ½ teaspoon sugar and ¼ teaspoon cinnamon. Bake at 425° for 15 minutes. Reduce oven temperature to 350°. Bake for 30 minutes. Yields 8 servings.

Cathy Martin, Birmingham South Council (Book 3)

Apple Pie

2 York apples, sliced
½ cup sugar
¼ teaspoon allspice
¼ teaspoon nutmeg

1 stick butter, softened
1 cup packed brown sugar
1 cup all-purpose flour

Arrange apple slices in a buttered pie plate. Sprinkle with sugar, allspice, and nutmeg. Cream butter in a mixer bowl until light and fluffy. Add brown sugar and flour; mix well. Spread over apple slices. Bake at 350° for 30 minutes. Yields 6–8 servings.

Elba Skinner, Selma Life Club (Book 4)

Baked "Fried" Apple Pies

1 (10-count) can butter-flavored
  biscuits
2 Delicious apples, peeled,
  finely chopped

Cinnamon to taste
½ cup butter, melted
1 cup sugar
2 cups Mellow Yellow soda

Roll out biscuits on floured surface. Spoon apples onto dough in equal amounts. Fold as for fried pies. Place in large baking pan. Sprinkle with cinnamon. Pour melted butter over all. Mix sugar and soda in bowl. Pour over pies. Bake at 350° for 35 minutes or until pastry is golden brown and apples are tender. Yields 10 servings.

Brenda Davis, Tuscaloosa Council (Book 3)

Easy Coconut Pie

2 eggs
1 cup sugar
¼ cup margarine, melted
1 (5-ounce) can evaporated
  milk

1 tablespoon vanilla extract
1 (3-ounce) can flaked coconut.
  divided
1 (9-inch) pie shell, unbaked

Cream eggs and sugar in mixer bowl until light and fluffy. Stir in margarine. Add evaporated milk, vanilla, and ¾ of coconut; mix well. Pour into pie shell. Sprinkle with remaining coconut. Bake at 350° for 30–45 minutes or until set. Yields 8 servings.

Martha S. Newsome, Phenix City Club (Book 3)

Coconut Caramel Pies

1 (7-ounce) package flaked
  coconut
1 cup chopped pecans
¾ stick margarine
1 (8-ounce) package cream
  cheese, softened
1 (14-ounce) can sweetened
  condensed milk

1 (16-ounce) container whipped
  topping
2 deep-dish graham cracker pie
  shells
1 (12-ounce) jar caramel ice
  cream topping

Cook coconut and pecans in margarine in a skillet until light brown, stirring constantly; drain well. Beat cream cheese and condensed milk in a mixing bowl until blended and smooth. Fold in whipped topping. Pour ¼ of the cream cheese mixture into each pie shell. Top each with ¼ of the coconut mixture. Drizzle each with ¼ of the caramel topping. Repeat layers. Freeze until firm. Serve frozen. Yields 12–16 servings.

Patsy Frost, Decatur Council (Book 4)

Coconut Pie

Makes its own crust.

4 eggs
½ cup self-rising flour
2 cups milk

1½ cups flaked coconut
1 teaspoon vanilla
1¾ cups sugar

Combine all ingredients in order given; mix well. Pour in well-greased, 10-inch glass pie pan and bake 45 minutes to 1 hour at 300°, until golden brown.

Rosemary Parker, Birmingham Central Council (Book 1)

Coconut Cream Pies

5 eggs, separated
1½ cups plus 10 tablespoons
sugar, divided
5 tablespoons all-purpose flour
3 cups milk

¼ cup butter
1 teaspoon vanilla extract
1 cup flaked coconut
2 (9-inch) pie shells, baked

Beat egg yolks; combine with 1½ cups sugar, flour, milk, and butter in double boiler. Cook until thickened, stirring frequently. Beat in vanilla. Stir in coconut. Pour into pie shells. Beat egg whites with remaining 10 tablespoons sugar in mixer bowl until stiff peaks form. Spread over filling, sealing to edge. Bake at 350° until golden brown. Yields 16 servings.

Margaret McHale, Birmingham Life Club (Book 3)

Low-Fat Fresh Strawberry Pie

2 cups fresh strawberries
1 (9-inch) pie shell, baked
1 cup sugar
¼ cup cornstarch

¼ cup strawberry gelatin
1 cup water
Whipped topping (optional)

Arrange strawberries in pie shell. Combine sugar, cornstarch, and gelatin in saucepan; mix well. Stir in water. Bring to a boil. Simmer until mixture coats spoon. Let stand to cool. Pour over strawberries. May top with whipped topping. Yields 8 servings.

Faye Carpenter and Martha L. Bryan, Huntsville Life Club
(Book 3)

Strawberry Margarita Pies

2 cups fresh strawberries
¼ cup sugar
¾ cup sweetened condensed
  milk
7 tablespoons tequila
6 tablespoons Triple Sec

1 tablespoon lime juice
1 (8-ounce) container whipped
  topping
2 (9-inch) graham cracker pie
  shells

Combine strawberries, sugar, condensed milk, tequila, Triple Sec, and lime juice in blender container. Process until puréed. Pour into large bowl. Fold in whipped topping. Pour into pie shells. Freeze, covered, overnight. May substitute 2 cups whipped cream for whipped topping. Yields 16 servings.

Mrs. A.T. Vaughn, Selma Life Club (Book 3)

West Gadsden Café
Strawberry Pie

1 (14-ounce) can sweetened
  condensed milk
1 (8-ounce) package cream
  cheese, softened
½ cup lemon juice

1 deep-dish pie shell, unbaked
⅓ cup sugar
¼ cup cornstarch
1 (16-ounce) package frozen
  strawberries

Cream condensed milk and cream cheese in a mixing bowl until light and fluffy. Stir in lemon juice. Pour into pie shell. Combine sugar, cornstarch, and strawberries in a saucepan. Cook until thickened, stirring frequently. Let stand until cool. Pour over pie. Chill until serving time. Yields 6–8 servings.

Kathryn Morgan, Gadsden Life Club (Book 4)

Key Lime Pie

5 eggs, separated
1 (14-ounce) can sweetened
  condensed milk
½ cup lime juice

1 (9-inch) graham cracker
  pie crust
10 tablespoons sugar

Stir egg yolks into condensed milk; add lime juice gradually, stirring as it is added. Pour into pie shell.

Beat egg whites gradually adding sugar until stiff peaks form; cover pie with meringue and bake at 325° for about 25 minutes or until brown.

Rosemary Parker, Birmingham Central Council (Book 2)

Quick Fruit Pie

1 cup all-purpose flour	¼ teaspoon salt
1 cup sugar	¾ stick butter, melted
1 cup milk	1 cup fruit of choice, drained

Mix first 5 ingredients; pour into deep-dish pie plate and pour fruit on top. Bake at 500° for 15–20 minutes.

Mrs. Buddy Gulledge, Anniston Council (Book 1)

Quick Pineapple Pie

1 (20-ounce) can crushed pineapple, well drained	1 cup chopped nuts
1 (14-ounce) can sweetened condensed milk	1 (8-ounce) carton whipped topping
⅓ cup lemon juice concentrate	2 graham cracker pie crusts
	Maraschino cherry halves or fresh strawberries for garnish

Combine pineapple, milk, lemon juice, and nuts. Fold in whipped topping. Pour into pie shells and refrigerate at least 2–3 hours. Garnish with cherries or strawberries before serving.

Eugenia Kite, Montgomery Council (Book 1)

Peaches and Cream Pie

3 cups chopped fresh peaches
1 (9-inch) deep-dish pie shell,
 unbaked
1½ cups sugar, divided
⅓ cup plus ½ cup all-purpose
 flour, divided

⅛ teaspoon salt
2 eggs, beaten
½ cup sour cream
¼ cup butter
1 fresh peach, sliced

Arrange chopped peaches in pie shell. Combine 1 cup sugar, ⅓ cup flour, and salt in bowl; mix well. Stir in eggs and sour cream. Spoon over peaches. Combine remaining ½ cup sugar and remaining ½ cup flour in bowl. Cut in butter until crumbly. Sprinkle evenly over pie. Bake at 350° for 1 hour or until golden brown. Top with peach slices. Yields 10 servings.

Oneda Webster, Decatur Council (Book 3)

Easy Fresh Peach Pie

3 eggs, separated
1 cup plus 6 tablespoons sugar,
 divided
3 tablespoons all-purpose flour

½ cup margarine, softened
1 cup sliced fresh peaches
1 (9-inch) pie shell, unbaked

Beat egg yolks in mixer bowl. Add 1 cup sugar, flour, and margarine, mixing well after each addition. Stir in peaches. Spoon into pie shell. Bake at 350° for 45 minutes or until set. Beat egg whites in mixer bowl until foamy. Add remaining 6 tablespoons sugar, beating constantly until sugar is dissolved. Spread over pie, sealing to edge. Bake until golden brown. Yields 6 servings.

Sandra Sims, Birmingham South Life Club (Book 3)

Pumpkin Chiffon Pie

3 envelopes unflavored gelatin
½ cup cold water
3 eggs, separated
1 cup sugar, divided
1¼ cups cooked pumpkin
½ teaspoon salt
½ teaspoon cinnamon
½ teaspoon ginger
¼ teaspoon nutmeg
½ teaspoon milk
1 (9-inch) pie shell, baked
Whipped cream and toasted
    coconut for garnish

Soften gelatin in cold water. Combine beaten egg yolks, ½ cup sugar, pumpkin, salt, cinnamon, ginger, nutmeg, and milk in double boiler. Cook over hot water until thickened. Stir in gelatin mixture. Let stand to cool completely. Beat egg whites until soft peaks form. Add remaining ½ cup sugar 1 tablespoon at a time, beating well after each addition. Fold in pumpkin mixture. Spoon into pie shell. Chill until serving time. Garnish with whipped cream and toasted coconut. Yields 8 serving.

Pauline Slusher, Birmingham Life Club (Book 3)

Sweet Potato Pie

2 cups mashed cooked sweet
    potatoes
3 eggs, lightly beaten
1 cup sugar
1 stick margarine, softened
1 teaspoon vanilla extract
1 teaspoon cinnamon
½–1 teaspoon nutmeg
Evaporated milk
1 (9-inch) pie shell, unbaked

Combine sweet potatoes, eggs, sugar, margarine, vanilla, cinnamon, and nutmeg in a bowl; mix well. Add enough evaporated milk to make the filling of desired consistency. Pour into pie shell. Bake at 350° for 1 hour or until set. Yields 6–8 servings.

Kathryn Morgan, Gadsden Life Club (Book 4)

Cheese Tarts

2 (8-ounce) packages cream
   cheese, softened
¾ cup sugar
3 eggs
1 package graham crackers,
   finely crushed

1 (8-ounce) carton sour cream
¼ teaspoon vanilla
1 or 2 tablespoons powdered
   sugar
1 (21-ounce) can cherry pie
   filling

Mix cream cheese, sugar, and eggs with beater or electric mixer until smooth. Put finely crushed graham crackers in mini muffin pan that has been well greased with margarine or shortening. Pour out excess crumbs.

Pour cream cheese mixture evenly into each cup. Bake at 300° for 12–14 minutes, until they rise. Let cool. Mix sour cream, vanilla, and powdered sugar to taste. Spoon small amount in center of each cup. Spoon cherry filling on top of sour cream mixture. May be served warm or chilled. May be frozen. Makes about 40.

Marcia Freeman, Birmingham East Council (Book 1)

Crusty Peach Cobbler

3 cups sliced peaches (canned or fresh)
¼ cup plus 3 tablespoons sugar, divided
1 tablespoon lemon juice
1 teaspoon grated lemon peel
1 teaspoon almond extract

1½ cups all-purpose flour
½ teaspoon salt
3 teaspoons baking powder
⅓ cup shortening
½ cup milk
1 egg, well beaten

Arrange peaches in a greased 8-inch square pan. Sprinkle with mixture of ¼ cup sugar, lemon juice, lemon peel, and almond extract. Heat in 375° oven while preparing shortcake.

Sift together flour, salt, baking powder, and 1 tablespoon sugar; cut in shortening until mixture is like coarse crumbs. Add milk and egg at once, and stir just until flour is moistened. Spread dough over hot peaches. Sprinkle with remaining 2 tablespoons sugar. Bake at 375° for 40 minutes.

Mrs. Mildred Clayton, Birmingham South Council (Book 1)

In 1978, American Telephone and Telegraph's (AT&T) Bell Laboratories began testing a mobile telephone system based on hexagonal geographical regions called cells. As the caller's vehicle passed from one cell to another, an automatic switching system would transfer the telephone call to another cell without interruption. The cellular telephone system began nationwide usage in the United States in 1983.

Blackberry Cobbler

1½ cups all-purpose flour
1 teaspoon baking powder
½ teaspoon salt
½ cup shortening
½ cup milk

3 cups blackberries
1 stick margarine
2 cups sugar
2 cups hot water

Combine flour, baking powder, and salt. Cut in shortening. Add milk and form dough. Roll out dough approximately ¼-inch thick. Place blackberries over dough and roll up like a jellyroll. Melt butter in a 9x13-inch baking pan. Cut dough into 1½-inch slices and place in pan. Dissolve sugar in hot water. Pour over dough slices in pan. Bake at 350° for 1–1¼ hours or until golden brown on top.

John Sumners, Birmingham South Council (Book 2)

Chocolate Cobbler

1 cup all-purpose flour
1¾ cups sugar, divided
¼ cup plus 1½ tablespoons
   baking cocoa, divided

½ cup milk
1 teaspoon vanilla extract
1 stick butter
1½ cups boiling water

Combine flour, ¾ cup sugar, 1½ tablespoons baking cocoa, milk, and vanilla in mixing bowl, and mix until well blended. Melt butter in a 9x13-inch baking pan. Pour batter into melted butter; do not stir. Mix remaining 1 cup sugar and ¼ cup cocoa in a small bowl and sprinkle over batter; do not stir. Drizzle boiling water over top; do not stir. Bake at 350° for 30 minutes. Serve warm. Yields 8–10 servings.

Judy Evans, Decatur Council (Book 4)

Sweet Potato Cobbler

2 large sweet potatoes	Dash of salt
2¼ cups water	⅓ teaspoon nutmeg
2 cups sugar	½ stick butter or margarine

Peel sweet potatoes and slice enough crosswise to measure about 3 cups. Combine sweet potatoes and water in a saucepan and simmer, covered, until tender. Drain sweet potatoes, reserving liquid. Combine reserved liquid, sugar, salt, and nutmeg and mix until sugar dissolves. Melt butter in a 9x13-inch baking dish. Add drained sweet potatoes. Add sugar mixture and arrange Pastry Strips over top. Bake at 350° for 35 minutes. Yields 8–10 servings.

PASTRY STRIPS:

¾ cup self-rising flour	3 tablespoons cold water
3 tablespoons vegetable oil	

Combine flour and oil in a bowl and mix until crumbly. Add water and mix until mixture forms a dough. Turn dough onto a lightly floured surface. Roll dough thinly and cut into 3-inch strips.

Mary Ann Sparks Fulmer, Shoals Life Club (Book 4)

Low-Fat Blueberry Cobbler

2 cups sugar, divided
1 tablespoon lemon juice
1 cup water

4 cups blueberries
1½ cups self-rising flour
½ cup butter

Combine 1 cup sugar, lemon juice, and water in bowl. Stir in blueberries. Spoon into buttered baking dish. Mix remaining 1 cup sugar and flour in bowl. Cut in butter until crumbly. Sprinkle over blueberry mixture. Bake at 350° until topping is brown. Yields 8 servings.

Maxine Pinckard (Mrs. Ken Pinckard), Montgomery Council
(Book 3)

Blueberry Crunch

1 (20-ounce) can juice-pack
  crushed pineapple
3 cups fresh or frozen
  blueberries
1 cup sugar, divided

1 (18¼-ounce) package yellow
  cake mix
½ cup butter, sliced
1 cup chopped pecans

Combine undrained pineapple, blueberries, and ¾ cup sugar in bowl; mix gently. Spread in buttered 9x13-inch baking dish. Sprinkle with cake mix; do not mix. Dot with butter; sprinkle with remaining ¼ cup sugar and pecans. Bake at 350° for 45 minutes. May make cuts with spoon to bottom of pan after 25 minutes baking time. Serve warm with whipped cream or ice cream. Yields 15 servings.

Mildred Hughes, Tuscaloosa Life Club/Louise Stringer, Mobile
Life Club (Book 3)

Blueberry Dessert

CRUST:

1 cup all-purpose flour   1 cup chopped nuts
1 stick margarine, softened

Mix all ingredients; press in baking dish. Bake for 20 minutes at 350°; let cool.

FILLING:

1 (8-ounce) package cream   1 (12-ounce) carton Cool Whip
  cheese, softened   ½ cup chopped nuts
1 cup sugar
1 (21-ounce) can blueberry
  pie filling

Mix cream cheese and sugar; put on top of Crust. Pour blueberry pie filling over cream cheese layer; put Cool Whip on top and sprinkle with nuts.

Cathy Porter, Tuscaloosa Council (Book 1)

Strawberry Dessert

1 (6-ounce) box French vanilla   1 (12-ounce) jar strawberry
  instant pudding mix   glaze
1 large angel food cake   1 (12-ounce) carton Cool Whip
1 quart strawberries

Use a 5-quart deep glass dish. Mix pudding as directed; let set for a few minutes to thicken. Crumble cake. Slice strawberries and mix with glaze. Make 2 layers of each: cake, pudding, Cool Whip, and strawberries. Chill thoroughly.

Hazel Campbell, Birmingham South Council (Book 1)

Apple Casserole

1½ (16-ounce) cans
    unsweetened sliced apples
1 cup shredded Cheddar
    cheese

½ cup butter, melted
1 cup sugar
¾ cup all-purpose flour
1 teaspoon vanilla extract

Spread apples in baking dish. Combine cheese, butter, sugar, flour, and vanilla in bowl; mix well. Spread over apples. Bake at 350° for 30 minutes or until light brown. May sprinkle top with additional cheese before baking, if desired. Yields 6 servings.

Mary C. Martin, Birmingham South Council (Book 3)

Oreo Cookie Dessert

1 (16-ounce) package Oreo
    cookies, crushed
½ cup margarine, melted
1 (8-ounce) package cream
    cheese, softened
½ cup sugar

1 (16-ounce) carton whipped
    topping
1 (6-ounce) package chocolate
    instant pudding mix
3 cups milk

Combine cookie crumbs and margarine in bowl; mix well. Press half the mixture into 9x13-inch dish. Combine cream cheese, sugar, and whipped topping in mixer bowl; beat until smooth. Spread over crumb layer. Combine pudding mix and milk in bowl; mix until thick. Spread over cream cheese layer. Sprinkle with remaining cookie crumb mixture. Chill until serving time. Yields 15 servings.

Bill "Moose" Benton, Birmingham South Council (Book 3)

Lemon Torte

PECAN CRUST:

1 stick butter, softened

1 cup all-purpose flour

1 cup chopped pecans

Beat butter in a mixing bowl until creamy. Add flour and pecans and mix until crumbly. Pat into a 9x13-inch baking dish. Bake at 350° for 20–25 minutes or until light brown. Let stand until completely cooled.

LEMON FILLING:

1 (8-ounce) package cream
  cheese, softened

1 (14-ounce) can sweetened
  condensed milk

⅓ cup lemon juice

1 (6-ounce) package lemon
  instant pudding mix

2½ cups cold milk

1 (8-ounce) carton whipped
  topping

Combine cream cheese, condensed milk, and lemon juice in a mixing bowl and beat until light and fluffy. Pour over cooled Pecan Crust. Prepare pudding mix with milk according to package directions. Spread over cream cheese layer. Top with whipped topping. Refrigerate until serving time. Yields 6–8 servings.

Betty C. Gray, Montgomery Life Club (Book 4)

Death by Chocolate

1 (18¼-ounce) package
  chocolate cake mix
1 cup crème de cocoa sauce
4 (4-ounce) packages chocolate
  mousse mix

24 ounces whipped topping
6 (2-ounce) Heath candy bars,
  crushed

Prepare and bake cake mix using package directions for 9x13-inch baking pan. Pierce cake with fork. Pour cocoa sauce over hot cake. Let stand for several minutes to overnight for sauce to soak in. Prepare mousse mix using package directions. Crumble cake. Layer cake pieces, mousse, whipped topping and candy ½ at a time in trifle bowl or 2 large dishes. Chill until serving time.

Variation: May substitute Skor bars for Heath bars. Yields 20 servings.

Mary C. Martin, Birmingham South Council (Book 3)

Chocolate Éclair

1 (1-pound) package graham
  crackers
2 (4-ounce) packages vanilla
  instant pudding mix

3 cups milk
8 ounces whipped topping
1 (16-ounce) can dark chocolate
  frosting

Arrange enough of the graham crackers to cover bottom of a 9x13-inch pan. Prepare pudding mixes with milk according to package directions. Fold in whipped topping. Spoon half the pudding mixture over graham crackers. Arrange another layer of graham crackers over pudding mixture. Add layers of remaining pudding mixture and graham crackers. Heat frosting in microwave for 1 minute to soften. Spread frosting over top. Refrigerate until serving time. Yields 8–10 servings.

Faye Grizzell, Birmingham South Life Club (Book 4)

Hot Dog Bun Pudding

1 cup raisins
2½ cups milk
2 cups sugar
1 stick margarine

6 eggs, beaten
1 teaspoon vanilla extract
1 package hot dog buns

Soak raisins in warm water to cover until plumped. Drain and set aside. Combine milk, sugar, and margarine in a saucepan. Heat until margarine melts and sugar is completely dissolved, stirring frequently. Stir a small amount of hot mixture into beaten eggs; stir eggs and vanilla into hot mixture. Split buns and arrange split side up in a 10x15-inch baking pan. Pour milk mixture over buns. Sprinkle raisins over top. Bake at 350° for 25–30 minutes or until golden brown and a knife inserted in center comes out clean. Yields 6 servings.

Hazel Campbell, Birmingham Life Club (Book 4)

Banana Pudding

2 (4-ounce) packages banana
  instant pudding mix
3 cups milk, divided
1 (14-ounce) can sweetened
  condensed milk

1 (16-ounce) container
  whipped topping
1 teaspoon vanilla extract
1 box vanilla wafers
6–8 bananas, sliced

Prepare banana pudding with 2 cups milk using package directions. Blend in condensed milk. Fold in whipped topping. Add remaining cup of milk and beat until well blended. Beat in vanilla. Crush several vanilla wafers for garnish, if desired. Alternate layers of vanilla wafers, pudding mixture, and bananas in a serving bowl until pudding is used. Garnish with a sprinkle of vanilla wafer crumbs. Yields 8–10 servings.

Mary Haynes, Birmingham South Cahaba Council (Book 4)

Old-Fashioned Banana Pudding

1½ cups sugar, divided
⅔ cup all-purpose flour
2 dashes salt
8 eggs, separated

4 cups milk
1 teaspoon vanilla extract
Vanilla wafers
7 or 8 large bananas, sliced

Combine 1 cup sugar, flour, and salt in top of a double boiler; mix well. Add beaten egg yolks and milk; mix well. Cook over boiling water until mixture thickens, stirring constantly. Reduce heat; cook 5 minutes longer, stirring frequently. Remove from heat and stir in vanilla. Spread a small amount of pudding over bottom of 3-quart baking dish. Add layers of vanilla wafers, banana slices and pudding ⅓ at a time. Beat egg whites until stiff but not dry peaks form. Add remaining ½ cup sugar gradually, beating constantly until very stiff peaks form. Spread over pudding, sealing to edge. Bake at 400° for 5 minutes or until golden brown. Yields 12 servings.

Virginia Greene, Birmingham South Life Club (Book 4)

Bread Pudding

11 slices bread, crumbled	5 eggs, separated
1 stick margarine, melted	1½ teaspoons vanilla extract
1½ cups sugar	Cinnamon and nutmeg to taste
2½ cups evaporated milk	Meringue
2½ cups milk	Sauce

Combine bread and margarine in a large mixing bowl; mix well. Add sugar, evaporated milk, milk, beaten egg yolks (save whites for Meringue), vanilla, cinnamon and nutmeg; mix well. Pour into a greased baking pan. Bake at 450° for 15 minutes. Spread Meringue over pudding, sealing to the edge. Bake 10 minutes longer or until golden brown. Pour warm Sauce over pudding.

MERINGUE:

5 egg whites	½ cup sugar

Beat egg whites in mixing bowl until soft peaks form. Add sugar 1 tablespoon at a time, beating constantly. Beat until stiff peaks form.

SAUCE:

1 cup evaporated milk	3 tablespoons margarine
1 cup milk	2 tablespoons vanilla or rum
1 cup sugar	extract
1½ tablespoons cornstarch	

Combine evaporated milk, milk, sugar, cornstarch, and margarine in a microwave-safe bowl. Microwave on HIGH for 4 minutes. Stir mixture well and rotate bowl about a half turn. Microwave for 4 minutes longer. Stir in extract. Yields 3 cups.

Faye Grizzell, Birmingham South Life Club (Book 4)

Egg Custard

⅔ cup sugar
5 eggs
2¼ cups milk

½ teaspoon salt
1 teaspoon vanilla
½ teaspoon nutmeg

Mix all ingredients except nutmeg in saucepan and heat until warm, then pour into glass baking dish. Sprinkle top with nutmeg. Put dish in a pan of water; bake at 350° for about 1 hour or until done.

Rosemary Parker, Birmingham Central Council (Book 2)

Amy's Ice Cream Sandwich Dessert

1 (16-ounce) carton whipped
  topping
⅓ cup Kahlúa

3 Skor candy bars
3 milk chocolate candy bars
24 ice cream sandwiches

Blend whipped topping and Kahlúa in a mixing bowl. Chop candy bars and mix them together. Arrange half the ice cream sandwiches in a 9x13-inch pan. Spread a layer of half the whipped topping mixture over the sandwiches and sprinkle with half the candy bar mixture. Repeat layers of ice cream sandwiches, whipped topping mixture, and candy bar mixture. Freeze for 6 hours or longer before serving. Yields 12 servings.

Virginia Greene, Birmingham South Life Club (Book 4)

Dessert Ice Cream Balls

½ cup raisins
Rum
½ gallon vanilla ice cream

2 cups toasted coconut, divided
½–¾ cup crushed pecans or
   almonds

Cover raisins with rum in a small bowl. Let stand about 15 minutes or until plumped. Drain raisins and discard rum. Place ice cream in a large bowl. Let stand until softened. Add raisins, 1 cup toasted coconut and pecans and mix well. Shape ice cream into balls about the size of a golf ball and roll in remaining toasted coconut to coat. Place ice cream balls in paper-lined muffin cups. Freeze until serving time. Yields about 2–2½ dozen balls.

Susan Robbins, Riverchase Council (Book 4)

No Egg Ice Cream

3 (14-ounce) cans sweetened
   condensed milk
2 tablespoons vanilla flavoring
Dash of salt

1 (21-ounce) can peach or
   strawberry pie filling
   (optional)
Milk to fill line

Place condensed milk, flavoring, salt, and pie filling, if desired, in 5-quart ice cream freezer. Add milk to fill line and stir until mixed with other ingredients. Freeze for 1–2 hours if firmer texture is desired; otherwise, may be eaten as soon as frozen.

Oris Bass (Book 1)

Strawberry Cheesecake Ice Cream

2 (8-ounce) packages cream
cheese, softened
2 cups sugar
3 eggs
1 (14-ounce) can sweetened
condensed milk

1 (12-ounce) can evaporated
milk
3 (10-ounce) packages frozen
strawberries, thawed
10 cups milk, divided

Beat cream cheese and sugar in mixer bowl until smooth. Add eggs; mix well. Stir in condensed milk, evaporated milk, strawberries, and 8 cups milk. Pour into 5-quart ice cream freezer container. Add remaining 2 cups milk or enough to fill to fill line. Freeze using manufacturer's instructions. Yields 20 servings.

Jean Spray, Huntsville Life Club (Book 3)

Equivalents, Substitutions, Etc.

EQUIVALENTS:

Apple: 1 medium = 1 cup chopped

Banana: 1 medium = ⅓ cup

Berries: 1 pint = 1¾ cups

Bread: 1 slice = ½ cup soft crumbs = ¼ cup fine, dry crumbs

Broth, beef or chicken: 1 cup = 1 bouillon cube dissolved in 1 cup boiling water

Butter: 1 stick = ¼ pound = ½ cup

Cabbage: 2 pounds = 9 cups shredded or 5 cups cooked

Cheese, grated: 1 pound = 4 cups; 8 ounces = 2 cups

Chicken: 1 large boned breast = 2 cups cooked meat

Chocolate, bitter: 1 square or 1 ounce = 2 tablespoons grated

Coconut: 3½-ounce can = 1⅓ cups

Cool Whip: 8 ounces = 3 cups

Cornmeal: 1 pound = 3 cups

Crabmeat, fresh: 1 pound = 3 cups

Crackers, graham: 15 = 1 cup crushed

Crackers, saltine: 23 = 1 cup crushed

Cream, heavy: 1 cup = 2–2½ cups whipped

Cream cheese: 3 ounces = 6⅔ tablespoons

Egg whites: 8–10 = 1 cup

Eggs: 4–5 = 1 cup

Evaporated milk: 5⅓-ounce can = ⅔ cup; 12-ounce can = 1¼ cups

Flour: 1 pound = 4½ cups

Flour, self-rising: 1 cup = 1 cup all-purpose + 1½ teaspoons baking powder + ½ teaspoon salt

Garlic powder: ⅛ teaspoon = 1 average clove

Gingerroot: 1 teaspoon = ¾ teaspoon ground

Grits: 1 cup = 4 cups cooked

Herbs, fresh: 1 tablespoon = 1 teaspoon dried

Lemon: 1 medium = 3 tablespoons juice

Marshmallows: ¼ pound = 16 large; ½ cup = 4 large

Milk, whole: 1 cup = ½ cup evaporated + ½ cup water

Mushrooms: ¼ pound fresh = 1 cup sliced

Mustard, dry: 1 teaspoon = 1 tablespoon prepared

Noodles: 1 pound = 7 cups cooked

Nuts, chopped: ¼ pound = 1 cup

Onion: 1 medium = ¾–1 cup chopped = 2 tablespoons dried chopped (flakes)

Orange: 3–4 medium = 1 cup juice

Pecans: 1 pound shelled = 4 cups

Potatoes: 1 pound = 3 medium

Rice: 1 cup = 3 cups cooked

Spaghetti: 1 pound uncooked = 5 cups cooked

Spinach, fresh: 2 cups chopped = 1 (10-ounce) package frozen chopped

Sugar, brown: 1 pound = 2½ cups

Sugar, powdered: 1 pound = 3½ cups

Sugar, white: 1 pound = 2¼ cups

Vanilla wafers: 22 = 1 cup fine crumbs

Equivalents, Substitutions, Etc.

SUBSTITUTIONS:

1 slice cooked bacon = 1 tablespoon bacon bits

1 cup buttermilk = 1 cup plain yogurt; or 1 tablespoon lemon juice or vinegar + plain milk to make 1 cup

1 cup sifted cake flour = $7/8$ cup sifted all-purpose flour

1 ounce unsweetened chocolate = 3 tablespoons cocoa + 1 tablespoon butter or margarine

1 ounce semisweet chocolate = 3 tablespoons cocoa + 1 tablespoon butter or margarine + 3 tablespoons sugar

1 tablespoon cornstarch = 2 tablespoons flour (for thickening)

1 cup heavy cream (for cooking, not whipping) = $1/3$ cup butter + $3/4$ cup milk

1 cup sour cream = $1/3$ cup milk + $1/3$ cup butter; or 1 cup plain yogurt

1 cup tartar sauce = 6 tablespoons mayonnaise or salad dressing + 2 tablespoons pickle relish

1 cup tomato juice = $1/2$ cup tomato sauce + $1/2$ cup water

1 cup vegetable oil = $1/2$ pound (2 sticks) butter

1 cup whipping cream, whipped = 6–8 ounces Cool Whip

1 cup whole milk = $1/2$ cup evaporated milk + $1/2$ cup water

MEASUREMENTS:

3 teaspoons = 1 tablespoon

1 tablespoon = $1/2$ fluid ounce

2 tablespoons = $1/8$ cup

3 tablespoons = 1 jigger

4 tablespoons = $1/4$ cup

8 tablespoons = $1/2$ cup or 4 ounces

12 tablespoons = $3/4$ cup

16 tablespoons = 1 cup or 8 ounces

$3/8$ cup = $1/4$ cup + 2 tablespoons

$5/8$ cup = $1/2$ cup + 2 tablespoons

$7/8$ cup = $3/4$ cup + 2 tablespoons

$1/2$ cup = 4 fluid ounces

1 cup = $1/2$ pint or 8 fluid ounces

2 cups = 1 pint or 16 fluid ounces

1 pint, liquid = 2 cups or 16 fluid ounces

1 quart, liquid = 2 pints or 4 cups

1 gallon, liquid = 4 quarts or 8 pints or 16 cups

OVEN-TO-CROCKPOT CONVERSIONS:

15–30 minutes in the oven = $1\frac{1}{2}$–$2\frac{1}{2}$ hours on HIGH or 4–6 hours on LOW

35–45 minutes in the oven = 2–3 hours on HIGH or 6–8 hours on LOW

50 minutes–3 hours in the oven = 4–5 hours on HIGH or 8–10 hours on LOW

Index

1983
Cellular

The development of commercial cellular systems did not occur rapidly—almost 36 years passed between the initial concept in 1947, and the first commercial systems in 1983. Delays due to regulatory discussions allowed developers to incorporate supporting technologies like microprocessors and integrated circuits into the cellular telephone as we know it. "Cellular" began as a term for analog service transferred from cell to cell, but now refers to all wireless phone services. Statistically, there were one million subscribers by 1987, increasing 1,000% by 1991 with both analog and digital capability. In 2008, there were more than 270 million wireless customers, who used more than 7.7 billion minutes per day.

Text messaging services appeared in 1993. Although "texting" started out slowly, it is now the most widely used and reliable mobile data service, with more than 3.5 billion text messages being sent out daily.

Index

Index

Index

Index

Index

Index

Index

Index

Index

Index

Index

Perfect gifts for any occasion.

Every recipe is a favorite, developed and perfected over generations of down-home cooking. This is a cookbook that will bring joy and great taste to every household.

**Best of the Best from
Calling All Cooks
Cookbook**

288 pages • 6x9 • Comb-bound
Index • $18.95 (shipping included)

All the classic cookbooks are still available!

**Calling All Cooks
(yellow)**

738 pages • 6x9 • Index
Paperbound • $12.00

**Calling All Cooks
Two (red)**

709 pages • 6x9 • Index
Paperbound • $12.00

**Calling All Cooks
Three (blue)**

646 pages • 6x9 • Index
Paperbound • $12.00

**Calling All Cooks
Four (green)**

575 pages • 6x9 • Index
Paperbound • $12.00

Phone: 1-205-321-1793

The new *Best of the Best from Calling All Cooks Cookbook,* along with the original *Calling All Cooks* cookbooks can be purchased directly from the Alabama Chapter of AT&T TelecomPioneers. They can be ordered by phone, or by using the order form on the following page.

Calling All Cooks
Order Form

❏ Check or money order enclosed

Charge to: ❏ Visa ❏ MC ❏ AmEx ❏ Disc

Card # _____

Expiration Date _____

Signature _____

Name _____

Address _____

_____

City/State/Zip _____

_____

Phone # _____

Email Address _____

Make check/money order payable to **Alabama Chapter #34** and send with Order Form to:
AT&T Telephone Pioneers
Chapter #34
600 N. 19th Street, 26th Floor
Birmingham, AL 35203

For more information: 1-205-321-1793

QTY.	TITLE	EACH	COST
	Best of the Best from Calling All Cooks	$18.95	
	Calling All Cooks (yellow)	$12.00	
	Calling All Cooks 2 (red)	$12.00	
	Calling All Cooks 3 (blue)	$12.00	
	Calling All Cooks 4 (green)	$12.00	
		TOTAL	

Note: U.S. currency only. Allow 6–8 weeks for delivery. Prices include postage and handling.

- -

Calling All Cooks
Order Form

❏ Check or money order enclosed

Charge to: ❏ Visa ❏ MC ❏ AmEx ❏ Disc

Card # _____

Expiration Date _____

Signature _____

Name _____

Address _____

_____

City/State/Zip _____

_____

Phone # _____

Email Address _____

Make check/money order payable to **Alabama Chapter #34** and send with Order Form to:
AT&T Telephone Pioneers
Chapter #34
600 N. 19th Street, 26th Floor
Birmingham, AL 35203

For more information: 1-205-321-1793

QTY.	TITLE	EACH	COST
	Best of the Best from Calling All Cooks	$18.95	
	Calling All Cooks (yellow)	$12.00	
	Calling All Cooks 2 (red)	$12.00	
	Calling All Cooks 3 (blue)	$12.00	
	Calling All Cooks 4 (green)	$12.00	
		TOTAL	

Note: U.S. currency only. Allow 6–8 weeks for delivery. Prices include postage and handling.

Collect the Series!
Best of the Best State Cookbook Series

Over 3.5 million copies sold! Cookbook collectors love this Series! The forty-two cookbooks, covering all fifty states (see previous page for listing), contain over 15,000 of the most popular local and regional recipes collected from approximately 3,000 of the leading cookbooks from these states.

To assist individuals who have purchased copies of the BEST OF THE BEST STATE COOKBOOKS and wish to collect the entire Series, we are offering a special **Collect the Series Discount.** You get:

- 25% discount off the list price ($16.95 minus 25% = $12.70 per copy).

- With a single order of five copies, you receive a sixth copy free. A single order of ten cookbooks gets two free copies, etc.

- ONLY $5.00 shipping cost for any number of books ordered (within contiguous United States).

- Order the entire 42-book Series for $395.00 plus $25.00 shipping. This represents another 10% savings off the Series discount.

Recipe Hall of Fame Cookbook Collection

  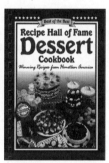

The Recipe Hall of Fame Cookbook	**The Recipe Hall of Fame Cookbook II**	**Quick & Easy Cookbook**	**Dessert Cookbook**
6x9 • 304 pages • Index Comb-bound • $16.95	6x9 • 304 pages • Index Comb-bound • $16.95	6x9 • 304 pages • Index Comb-bound • $16.95	6x9 • 240 pages • Index Comb-bound • $16.95

Special Offer! Four-book collection for $40

Collect the Series discounts (see above) also apply to the RECIPE HALL OF FAME COLLECTION. These cookbooks can be ordered for $12.70 per copy (25% discount) or $40.00 for four-book set (40% discount). Shipping is only $5.00 for any number of books ordered. To order online, enter coupon code 4FAME.

Individuals may order cookbooks by phone, mail, or online. All major credit cards accepted. Be sure to mention **Collect the Series** special discount.

QUAIL RIDGE PRESS
P. O. Box 123 • Brandon, MS 39043 • 1-800-343-1583
info@quailridge.com • www.quailridge.com
www.facebook.com/cookbookladies • cookbookladies.blogspot.com

BEST OF THE BEST STATE COOKBOOK SERIES

ALABAMA	HAWAII	MINNESOTA	OREGON
ALASKA	IDAHO	MISSISSIPPI	PENNSYLVANIA
ARIZONA	ILLINOIS	MISSOURI	SO. CAROLINA
ARKANSAS	INDIANA	NEVADA	TENNESSEE
BIG SKY *Includes Montana, Wyoming*	IOWA	NEW ENGLAND *Includes Rhode Island,*	TEXAS
CALIFORNIA	KENTUCKY	*Connecticut, Massachusetts,*	TEXAS II
COLORADO	LOUISIANA	*Vermont, New Hampshire,* *and Maine*	UTAH
FLORIDA	LOUISIANA II	NEW MEXICO	VIRGINIA
GEORGIA	MICHIGAN	NEW YORK	VIRGINIA II
GREAT PLAINS *Includes North Dakota,* *South Dakota, Nebraska,* *and Kansas*	MID-ATLANTIC *Includes Maryland,* *Delaware, New Jersey, and* *Washington, D.C.*	NO. CAROLINA OHIO OKLAHOMA	WASHINGTON WEST VIRGINIA WISCONSIN

All BEST OF THE BEST COOKBOOKS are 6x9 inches, are comb-bound, contain approximately 400 recipes, and total 264–352 pages. Each contains illustrations, photographs, an index, and a list of contributing cookbooks, a special feature that cookbook collectors enjoy. Interesting information about each state is scattered throughout the cookbooks, including historical facts and major attractions along with amusing trivia. Retail price per copy: $16.95.

See previous page for special Collect the Series Discounts.

To order by credit card, call toll-free **1-800-343-1583**, visit **www.quailridge.com**, or use the Order Form below.

Order Form

Send check, money order, or credit card info to:
QUAIL RIDGE PRESS • P. O. Box 123 • Brandon, MS 39043

Name _____

Address _____

City _____

State/Zip _____

Phone # _____

Email Address _____

❑ Check enclosed

Charge to: ❑ Visa ❑ MC ❑ AmEx ❑ Disc

Card # _____

Expiration Date _____

Signature _____

Qty.	Title of Book (or State) (or Set)	Total

Subtotal _____

Mississippi residents add 7% sales tax _____

Postage (any number of books) + $5.00

TOTAL _____